Devotions on the
Greek New Testament

Devotions on the
Greek New Testament

52 REFLECTIONS TO INSPIRE & INSTRUCT

J. Scott Duvall & Verlyn D. Verbrugge, editors

ZONDERVAN

Devotions on the Greek New Testament
Copyright © 2012 by J. Scott Duvall

Requests for information should be addressed to:
Zondervan, 3900 *Sparks Dr. SE, Grand Rapids, Michigan 49546*

Library of Congress Cataloging-in-Publication Data

    Devotions on the Greek New Testament / J. Scott Duvall and Verlyn D.
Verbrugge, general editors.
        p. cm.
    Includes bibliographical references and index.
    ISBN 978-0-310-49254-2 (softcover)
    1. Bible. N.T. Greek—Versions. 2. Bible. N.T.—Meditations. I. Duvall, J.
Scott. II. Verbrugge, Verlyn D.
    BS1938.D48 2012
    242'.5—dc23   2012002698

Cover design: Mark Novell:, www.imagocommunity.com
Cover photography: The Center for the Study of New Testament Manuscripts,
        www.csntm.org
Interior design: Matthew Van Zomeren

Printed in the United States of America

14 15 16 17 18 19 20 /DCI/ 20 19 18 17 16 15 14 13 12 11 10 9 8 7 6 5 4 3

Contents

Introduction

One of the common questions students wonder about when they are doing Greek exegesis in class is whether they will be able to keep it up as they enter a busy ministry. Moreover, they ask themselves, *Does it really make a difference in the understanding and application of the Bible? What can you gain from reading a passage in Greek that you cannot gain from an English translation?*

The need to know why you are studying Greek, particularly in relation to the ultimate purpose of strengthening your walk with the Lord, never fades into the background. With that purpose in mind, we have edited and contributed to *Devotions on the Greek New Testament* to help students (and professors) keep their study of Greek a deeply *Spirit*ual experience.

The book includes fifty-two short devotions drawn from select passages throughout the Greek New Testament. A diverse group of authors, all experts in the area of New Testament Greek exegesis, offer a varied collection of devotions. Some insights focus on particular words and their role in the passage, while others highlight background studies or provide a theological reading of the passage. Some contributions diagram the passage, others trace important literary patterns such as chiasms, and still others draw attention to the connections between the Old and New Testaments. Each devotion draws students into translating a short passage and understanding why this or that insight matters greatly for our life and ministry.

We hope that *Devotions* will help motivate you to endure in your Greek studies. Alongside first-class grammars, vocabulary guides, and handbooks on exegesis, this short collection of devotions will go a long way toward keeping you in the game. One of the most formidable tasks teachers face in a Facebook and Twitter world is keeping student interest and motivation high. In this book, you will find a friend and ally in this important task.

The often-quoted dictum printed in the preface to Johannes Albrecht Bengel's 1734 edition of the Greek New Testament remains as true today as it was then: "Apply yourself totally to the text; apply the text totally to yourself." We offer this small contribution to this larger kingdom purpose of knowing and loving our Lord Jesus Christ.

J. Scott Duvall and Verlyn D. Verbrugge,
editors and contributors

Scott Duvall actually proposed this book on Greek devotions about seven years ago. At that time Zondervan was building its library of basic Greek resources for first and second year Greek, and Zondervan is proud of the authors who have written so many resources that have become the standard in colleges and seminaries. But at that time, we did not focus on students keeping their Greek as they left their schools to become pastors and teachers.

That time has come. When I asked Scott if he might now be able to undertake this project, he was in the middle of several significant writing projects. So I suggested that perhaps as editor at Zondervan, I could partner with him on helping with the busy work of contacting scholars to submit contributions. I could not ask for a better working relationship with an author/scholar to put together this set of devotions, and we are thankful to God that this book has now been published.

Verlyn D. Verbrugge

I was pleasantly surprised when Verlyn suggested that Zondervan was interested in revisiting the book on Greek devotions. Working with Verlyn has been an honor and a privilege. His linguistic expertise is top-tier and he uses his gifts as a scholar/pastor to draw people closer to Christ. He has done more than his fair share of work on the project, including contacting potential authors, giving careful editorial attention to the contributions, and coordinating much of the work. In short, the book would not have been published apart from Verlyn's significant involvement. I'm deeply grateful for the opportunity to coedit this small volume with Verlyn Verbrugge, a servant of Christ whom I greatly respect.

J. Scott Duvall

Learning from Joseph's Righteousness
MATTHEW 1:19

Ἰωσὴφ δὲ ὁ ἀνὴρ αὐτῆς, δίκαιος ὢν καὶ μὴ θέλων αὐτὴν δειγματίσαι, ἐβουλήθη λάθρᾳ ἀπολῦσαι αὐτήν.

What does biblical righteousness look like in practice? When confronted with what appeared to be a clear case of unfaithfulness on the part of his betrothed, Joseph decides to divorce her quietly. Matthew 1:19 indicates two key factors (besides the presumption of Mary's guilt) that help us understand his plan for dealing with the issue. These two factors are indicated in two participles that appear between the opening reference to Joseph as Mary's husband and the final clause, which contains the main verb and tells us his decision.

The relevant participles could be translated "being righteous [δίκαιος ὢν] and not wanting [μὴ θέλων] to make an example of her." But these participles can be understood in more than one way, and the English translation just given does not offer the same variety of interpretations as the Greek. Most interpreters take both participles to be causal — Joseph acted as he did *because* he was righteous and did not want to make a public example of Mary by denouncing her as an immoral woman. Some, however, argue that since both Roman law and Jewish tradition were clear that righteousness required the public denouncement of unfaithfulness, lest the innocent party be guilty of condoning or covering up sin in the community, the first participle should be taken as concessive (i.e., "despite being righteous and because he was unwilling to make an example of her, he decided ...").

One's perception of the logical relationship between the nature of righteousness and Joseph's plan depends to a great extent on one's understanding of the nature of righteousness. While it is true that Roman and Jewish legal traditions required the exposure of sexual unfaithfulness, the text clearly presents Joseph both as righteous *and* unwilling to subject Mary to public denouncement. The present participle indicates not that he had been righteous but thought of acting unrighteously in this instance, but rather that he was righteous even as he decided on his plan of action. The only question is whether his decision was unexpected in the light of his righteousness (if the participle is taken to be concessive) or was a direct result of his righteousness (if it is taken to be causal). I suggest that while the parallel participles would tend to suggest that both should be taken as causal, the question is one that will be clarified as readers make their way through the rest of the gospel.

The gospel of Matthew seeks to transform our understanding of the true nature of righteousness in light of its redefinition by Jesus and by Matthew's telling of his story. In this gospel it becomes clear that for Jesus (and Matthew), mercy and compassion are not at odds with righteousness, but are crucial marks *of* righteousness, just as they are in the Old Testament. Jesus demands not the same righteousness as the scribes and Pharisees but a greater righteousness (5:20), one that will lead his disciples to show mercy to the least of his brothers (25:34–40). Jesus emphasized the theme of Hosea 6:6: God prefers mercy over sacrifice (Matt. 9:13; 12:7), and he demonstrated what that preference looks like by befriending tax collectors and sinners. His sacrifice on the cross is about extending mercy to us sinners rather than leaving us to our own destruction.

By the time we finish Matthew's gospel, it is clear that even if

Joseph's plan seemed unexpected according to traditional percep-
tions of righteousness, it was what one would expect in the light
of the transformed understanding of righteousness taught and
modeled by Jesus himself. It was that kind of righteousness that
led Joseph to think and act as he did.

Roy E. Ciampa

Extending Jesus

Καὶ περιῆγεν ἐν ὅλῃ τῇ Γαλιλαίᾳ, διδάσκων ἐν ταῖς συναγωγαῖς αὐτῶν καὶ κηρύσσων τὸ εὐαγγέλιον τῆς βασιλείας καὶ θεραπεύων πᾶσαν νόσον καὶ πᾶσαν μαλακίαν ἐν τῷ λαῷ.

Καὶ περιῆγεν ὁ Ἰησοῦς τὰς πόλεις πάσας καὶ τὰς κώμας, διδάσκων ἐν ταῖς συναγωγαῖς αὐτῶν καὶ κηρύσσων τὸ εὐαγγέλιον τῆς βασιλείας καὶ θεραπεύων πᾶσαν νόσον καὶ πᾶσαν μαλακίαν.

Καὶ προσκαλεσάμενος τοὺς δώδεκα μαθητὰς αὐτοῦ ἔδωκεν αὐτοῖς ἐξουσίαν πνευμάτων ἀκαθάρτων ὥστε ἐκβάλλειν αὐτὰ καὶ θεραπεύειν πᾶσαν νόσον καὶ πᾶσαν μαλακίαν.... πορευόμενοι δὲ κηρύσσετε λέγοντες ὅτι Ἤγγικεν ἡ βασιλεία τῶν οὐρανῶν.

Matthew did not divide up his gospel into verses or chapters, nor did any of his contemporaries divide up their writings. Sometimes ancient authors indicated "sections" by using repetition. Our texts repeat three different verbs (διδάσκω, κηρύσσω, and θεραπεύω) and several distinctive nouns that together reveal how we should read Matthew 4:23–11:1. We must pay attention to these verbs and nouns.

In 4:23 notice how Matthew describes the mission of Jesus with three present participles designed to make vivid before our eyes what Jesus is doing:

διδάσκων ἐν ταῖς συναγωγαῖς αὐτῶν καὶ

κηρύσσων τὸ εὐαγγέλιον τῆς βασιλείας καὶ

θεραπεύων πᾶσαν νόσον καὶ πᾶσαν μαλακίαν ἐν τῷ λαῷ

Notice, then, how 9:35 closes with an almost exact repetition of that description of his mission:

διδάσκων ἐν ταῖς συναγωγαῖς αὐτῶν καὶ
κηρύσσων τὸ εὐαγγέλιον τῆς βασιλείας καὶ
θεραπεύων πᾶσαν νόσον καὶ πᾶσαν μαλακίαν.

Finally, notice the astounding move made next in 10:1, 7: the twelve missioners of Jesus are sent out to do *the very same things minus one: teaching.*

θεραπεύειν πᾶσαν νόσον καὶ πᾶσαν μαλακίαν
πορευόμενοι δὲ **κηρύσσετε** λέγοντες

Observation of these Greek texts leads us to several important strategies for reading Matthew 4:23–11:1. First, Jesus' mission in 4:23 is threefold: he teaches in synagogues, he preaches the good news of the kingdom, and he heals people.

Second, since 9:35 again describes Jesus' threefold mission, we can argue that chapters 5–7 describe Jesus' mission of teaching (imparting information) and preaching (announcing good news) and chapters 8–9 his mission of healing (Jesus heals ten times in those two chapters). Even if we were to argue that the healing chapters are also about preaching, the point remains the same: Jesus' mission is threefold.

Third, Matthew's language and repetition of verbs and nouns in 10:1, 7 reveal that Matthew wants his readers to see that *what Jesus did* in chapters 5–9 is what he wants his followers to do (9:36–11:1 comprising the mission discourse). They are to *heal* people of "every disease and sickness," as did Jesus, and they are to "preach" the good news (10:7, their message being the same as John's and Jesus'; cf. 3:2; 4:17). The fundamental download for us today is to see that "our" ministries are not ours. They are none other than Jesus' ministry, and our calling is to extend Jesus and Jesus' ministry into the world.

But why is "teaching" missing from chapter 10? Surely Matthew, as careful a writer as he was, did not forget that Jesus also taught (4:23; 9:35). Most likely the omission is a result of Jesus' knowing that the disciples were not yet sufficiently informed to be teachers. So they must be prepared. Though Jesus does indicate that someday his disciples will teach (cf. 13:51–52), it is not until his full teaching has been explained, his Passion has been endured, his resurrection has been experienced, and his ascension is about to occur that he finally tells his disciples they are to be teachers—teaching what Jesus commanded (28:16–20).

Scot McKnight

Jesus and the Law and Prophets

MATTHEW 5:17–20

Μὴ νομίσητε ὅτι ἦλθον καταλῦσαι τὸν νόμον ἢ τοὺς προφήτας·
οὐκ ἦλθον καταλῦσαι ἀλλὰ πληρῶσαι. ἀμὴν γὰρ λέγω ὑμῖν,
ἕως ἂν παρέλθῃ ὁ οὐρανὸς καὶ ἡ γῆ, ἰῶτα ἓν ἢ μία κεραία οὐ
μὴ παρέλθῃ ἀπὸ τοῦ νόμου ἕως ἂν πάντα γένηται. ὃς ἐὰν οὖν
λύσῃ μίαν τῶν ἐντολῶν τούτων τῶν ἐλαχίστων καὶ διδάξῃ οὕτως
τοὺς ἀνθρώπους, ἐλάχιστος κληθήσεται ἐν τῇ βασιλείᾳ τῶν
οὐρανῶν· ὃς δ᾽ ἂν ποιήσῃ καὶ διδάξῃ, οὗτος μέγας κληθήσεται ἐν
τῇ βασιλείᾳ τῶν οὐρανῶν. λέγω γὰρ ὑμῖν ὅτι ἐὰν μὴ περισσεύσῃ
ὑμῶν ἡ δικαιοσύνη πλεῖον τῶν γραμματέων καὶ Φαρισαίων, οὐ μὴ
εἰσέλθητε εἰς τὴν βασιλείαν τῶν οὐρανῶν.

In clear, terse, and potent language, Jesus clarifies his posture
toward the Torah and reveals how we are to live in the age of
fulfillment. Our discipleship is rooted in a singular claim: Jesus
is the messianic completion of the entire history of God's ways
with Israel (the Law and the Prophets). Discipleship is about living under the teachings of the Messiah.

Jesus makes an astounding claim here. His use of aorist
tenses (νομίσητε, ἦλθον καταλῦσαι [2x], πληρῶσαι) in verse 17
captures the major actions in four simple photos: "think," "came
to destroy" (twice), "fulfill." These verbal forms are summary
aorists (aorists that capture action as a whole), which together
make one profound point: Jesus *brings to completion* everything

the Torah said (and tried to say) and everything the Prophets said and predicted. (The verb πληρόω is important to Matthew's understanding of how to connect Israel's story to Jesus [see 1:22; 2:15, 17, 23; 3:15; 4:14].)

Jesus' claim is *rooted in Scripture*. What verse 18 teaches is not that the Torah is permanent and unchangeable as originally given, but the Torah (and the Prophets) are permanent *as fulfilled in Jesus Christ*. That is, those who truly follow Jesus do all that the Torah and the Prophets want for God's people. This posture of Jesus does not undermine Torah observance but *expands* obedience to its fullest proportions. The ἕως clause of verse 18 logically follows the ἰῶτα clause so we can reconfigure the logic in this way: not a dot or a dash will pass from the Torah (no Prophets this time) as long as heaven and earth exist. The second ἕως clause encapsulates the first one: heaven and earth's passing away is the same as "until everything is accomplished."

Jesus' claim shapes discipleship. Our passage moves logically from a powerful gospel claim (Jesus fulfills the whole lot!) to potent implications for how to follow Jesus as gospel-ized people. The simple inferential οὖν clarifies how we are to live out Jesus' moral vision. Jesus outlines two categories of people. (1) Some loosen and teach (aorist subjunctives here emphasize contingency and simple action conceived as a whole) anything other than the fullness of God's way; they will be called "least." If we examine the term "least" in Matthew's gospel, we will conclude that "least" is a nice way of saying "condemned" (e.g., 13:47 – 50; 22:1 – 14). (2) Others do and teach (also aorist subjunctives to emphasize conditionality); they will be called "great" (eternally approved by God).

Discipleship means separation. Since final judgment is connected to one's observance of the Torah *as fulfilled in Jesus*, one's "righteousness" (i.e., observance of God's will as taught by Jesus) must transcend ("*greatly* [πλεῖον] exceed") that of the Pharisees and scribes, whose "righteousness" is Moses-alone, not the Jesus form of the Torah. Jesus is calling his followers to follow his teachings, not those of the scribes and Pharisees.

It's all about Jesus. He fulfills the whole story, and that means his followers walk on a path walked by the Messiah.

Scot McKnight

The Great Commission
MATTHEW 28:19–20A

Πορευθέντες οὖν μαθητεύσατε πάντα τὰ ἔθνη, βαπτίζοντες αὐτοὺς εἰς τὸ ὄνομα τοῦ πατρὸς καὶ τοῦ υἱοῦ καὶ τοῦ ἁγίου πνεύματος, διδάσκοντες αὐτοὺς τηρεῖν πάντα ὅσα ἐνετειλάμην ὑμῖν.

"Therefore go and make disciples of all nations, baptizing them in the name of the Father and of the Son and of the Holy Spirit, and teaching them to obey everything I have commanded you" (Matt. 28:19-20a, NIV). Virtually every major and not a few minor English translations render the first two verbs in this sentence as commands: "go" and "make." Of all the more recent English translations, only the God's Word translation reads, "So wherever you go, make disciples of all nations."

Countless preachers and other speakers at missionary meetings and conferences, however, make the point that in the Greek, only "make disciples" (μαθητεύσατε) is in the imperative mood. "Go" translates an aorist deponent passive participle (πορευθέντες, literally "when you go"). Its verbal impact is not as heavily marked as that of the aorist imperative. Why, then, do most modern English translations render both verbs as commands?

Some commentators have referred to πορευθέντες as an imperatival participle, but that label should be reserved for the rare appearances of a participle unconnected to any finite verb. The participle here is best understood as one of attendant circumstances—a participle loosely attached to the main verb of

24

the sentence. While grammatically subordinate to the main verb, such participles remain conceptually coordinate. In other words, they can be translated as equivalent in mood to the verbs they modify. Since the main verb of this sentence is an imperative, a participle of attendant circumstances modifying it also takes on some imperative sense and may be translated accordingly. This case particularly applies when the participle precedes the verb it modifies, as it does here.

Thus both "camps" are correct. "Make disciples" remains the most central command of the sentence, but "go" can be translated equally well via an imperative as via a participle. Where are we called to go? Anywhere there are people in need of hearing the gospel, being baptized, or being taught to observe all of Christ's teachings. Some will indeed travel cross-culturally, even to "the ends of the earth" (Acts 1:8), but others will have to witness to friends, neighbors, and family members close by.

The present participles "baptizing" and "teaching," by contrast, are not as likely to reflect the imperatival nuance, though again their modifying the imperative μαθητεύσατε means that they will be tinged with this sense. More likely they are modal or instrumental participles, helping to describe the manner or means, respectively, by which the twelve apostles and those who follow them will evangelize the people groups of the entire world. If, as a few grammarians suggest, there is such a thing as a consecutive participle (i.e., of result), "baptizing" and "teaching" could also carry that nuance. But the dubiousness of this participial category makes that nuance of meaning less certain than the other two options.

In some ages and in some parts of the world today, Christians have believed that this "Great Commission" was not intended for all believers, but only for the Twelve. They then try not to press all Christians to be winsome witnesses to their faith. But this interpretation runs afoul of a simple observation: Christ commanded his disciples to teach the nations *everything* he had taught them. "Everything" clearly includes the Great Commission, so by definition, to be faithful in obeying Matthew 28:19–20a each person will witness to whomever will listen in order to ensure that Christianity remains throughout the generations still to come.

Craig L. Blomberg

Holy One of God

Τί ἡμῖν καὶ σοί, Ἰησοῦ Ναζαρηνέ; ἦλθες ἀπολέσαι ἡμᾶς; οἶδά σε τίς εἶ, ὁ ἅγιος τοῦ θεοῦ.

Jesus' first miracle in the gospel of Mark (1:21–28) is a "power encounter" between Jesus and an unclean spirit. The people in the synagogue probably thought that the demon had won a significant victory over Jesus when it addressed Jesus by his full name and even a secret title; but Jesus quickly silenced the demon and sent it away. Jesus' quick and powerful exorcism forced the witnesses to ask a question: "What is this? A new teaching with authority!" (1:27).

The gospel of Mark is a biography, and as we read this gospel, we must keep one question front and center: "Who is Jesus?" In the middle of this episode in Mark 1, the unclean spirit offers one answer to that question of identity: Jesus of Nazareth is ὁ ἅγιος τοῦ θεοῦ ("the Holy One of God"). What does that title mean? Casual readers may assume that refers to Jesus' deity or to his holiness. But while Jesus' deity is important, even central, Mark is often interested in pointing to other aspects of Jesus' identity.

The title ὁ ἅγιος τοῦ θεοῦ is not common in the Scriptures; it occurs only two other times in the New Testament (Luke 4:34; John 6:69). As with most of Jesus' titles, the key to understanding them is found in the Old Testament. In the Septuagint, the Greek Old Testament, three important leaders of Israel receive the title "holy one of God." Aaron, the first high priest, was called τὸν ἅγιον κυρίου ("the holy one of the LORD") in Psalm 106:16. When Samson was asked about the source of his strength, he replied (in the Hebrew Bible) that it resulted from his being a "Nazirite of God"; the Septuagint translates this answer as ἅγιος θεοῦ (Judg. 16:17). And in 2 Kings 4:9 the great prophet Elisha was called θεοῦ ἅγιος.

Why were these three individuals identified as "holy one[s] of God"? Aaron, Samson, and Elisha were each appointed, protected, and empowered by God. Aaron was called "the holy one of the LORD" in contrast to the rebellious sons of Korah; God protected Aaron's priestly position by destroying the would-be usurpers (Ps. 106:16–18; cf. Num. 16:1–33). Samson was a great rescuer; although morally flawed, he was able to destroy the enemies of God's people because he was God's "holy one." Elisha and Elijah were unique among the prophets in that they not only pronounced the blessings and curses of the covenant, but also personally enacted those blessings and curses. Elisha was given the title "holy one of God" in the context of bringing miraculous blessings such as multiplying food, bringing fruitfulness to the womb of a barren woman, and raising a child from the dead (2 Kings 4).

The title "Holy One of God" was thus especially suited to Jesus. The demon feared "the Holy One" because he knew that Jesus was appointed, empowered, and protected by God. Like God's appointed "holy ones" of the past, Jesus was under God's protection, defeated the enemies of God's people, and brought the blessings of healing and provision to God's people.

The title that terrified the unclean spirit is the same title that comforts and inspires followers of Jesus of Nazareth. Jesus is the Holy One of God, the great rescuer. He continues to defeat the power of sin and brings God's blessings to his people, and no power on the earth or under it can oppose him—or them.

Gary Manning Jr.

Jesus Heals the Paralytic

MARK 2:3–5A

Καὶ ἔρχονται φέροντες πρὸς αὐτὸν παραλυτικὸν αἰρόμενον ὑπὸ τεσσάρων. καὶ μὴ δυνάμενοι προσενέγκαι αὐτῷ διὰ τὸν ὄχλον ἀπεστέγασαν τὴν στέγην ὅπου ἦν, καὶ ἐξορύξαντες χαλῶσι τὸν κράβαττον ὅπου ὁ παραλυτικὸς κατέκειτο. καὶ ἰδὼν ὁ Ἰησοῦς τὴν πίστιν αὐτῶν.

Have you heard a sermon about the healing of the paralytic in which the preacher highlights the "faith of the four" and encourages the congregation to act "in faith" in order to receive healing? While faith is noted in this passage, faith is not its primary focus. Mark's word order and choice of vocabulary point in a different direction.

In this narrative, so many gather in the Capernaum home where Jesus is speaking that there is no room to enter (2:1–2). Mark describes the action of the four men "bringing" the paralytic to Jesus in what might seem to be a rough style of writing: "They came, *bearing* to him a paralytic *taken up* by four, and not being able *to bring* to him on account of the crowd they unroofed the roof where he was" (2:3–4a, lit. trans.). In this sentence, the author places his phrases in a particular order and chooses vocabulary for the purpose of pointing the reader to the person of Christ.

In verse 3, Mark could have focused on "the four men" as the actors in this story by referring to them in the nominative case and drawing attention to them by putting something like καὶ τέσσαρες ἄνθρωποι first in the sentence; instead, Mark chooses to deemphasize the *persons* doing the action by referring to them in a prepositional phrase ("by four [men]") after a passive participle (αἰρόμενον) at the end of the sentence. In doing so, he accents their *action*—"bearing," "taking up," and "bringing."

The last verbal idea in this series, "bringing" (προσενέγκαι, from προσφέρω), is a word that Mark rarely uses (see 1:44; 10:13) but one that has rich theological meaning. In a similar manner, Matthew uses προσφέρω to refer to the act of bringing a sick person to Jesus (Matt 8:16), but he also chooses this word to intend the act of "offering" or "presenting a gift" as an act of worship (e.g., Matt 2:11; 5:23–24). Not only does this use reflect a common Greco-Roman sense of the word, but also the overwhelming number of occurrences of προσφέρω in the Septuagint, particularly in Leviticus and Numbers, connote a sacrificial sense. Since Mark writes years after the healing event and since he understands the relevance of the death and resurrection of Jesus (keep in mind the belief in biblical times that sickness was a result of sin), Mark's synonyms stress *to whom* the men are seeking to "present" (προσφέρω) the paralytic—the One who has authority to heal and forgive.

Moreover, notice how the verbal ideas in verses 3–4 lead the reader to focus on the person of Christ: "they came bearing *to him* [πρὸς αὐτὸν] ... not able to bring *to him* [αὐτῷ] they unroofed the roof *where he was* [ὅπου ἦν]." It is not surprising, then, that Mark highlights the action of Jesus in "seeing" their faith by placing the participle "seeing" first in the sentence (2:5a). After "seeing," Jesus pronounces forgiveness and heals the paralytic.

Mark's description and arrangement in these few verses help us understand an important theological point: the focus of Mark is not on the faith of people or on the decisions of people but on bringing needs *to the person of Jesus*. While the faith of the friends remains an important aspect in Mark's narrative, the primacy of place goes to Jesus as the great Healer. With his redemptive and powerful character, it is he who deserves our worship.

David Wallace

Discovering the Main Verb

καὶ γυνὴ οὖσα ἐν ῥύσει αἵματος δώδεκα ἔτη καὶ πολλὰ παθοῦσα ὑπὸ πολλῶν ἰατρῶν καὶ δαπανήσασα τὰ παρ' αὐτῆς πάντα καὶ μηδὲν ὠφεληθεῖσα ἀλλὰ μᾶλλον εἰς τὸ χεῖρον ἐλθοῦσα, ἀκούσασα περὶ τοῦ Ἰησοῦ, ἐλθοῦσα ἐν τῷ ὄχλῳ ὄπισθεν ἥψατο τοῦ ἱματίου αὐτοῦ.

If you use only English translations to form your understanding of Scripture, you will frequently miss some of the subtle messages communicated by the inspired authors of the Bible. Mark 5:25–27 offers a case in point; this group of verses appears to consist of three independent sentences that rehearse the story of a hemorrhaging woman.

> And a woman was there who had been subject to bleeding for twelve years. She had suffered a great deal under the care of many doctors and had spent all she had, yet instead of getting better she grew worse. When she heard about Jesus, she came up behind him in the crowd and touched his cloak.

Reading this NIV translation makes it practically impossible to discern whether the author is emphasizing any particular detail in the narrative. Looking at the Greek, however, changes the picture significantly. English versions often translate participles as main verbs. Can you spot all the aorist participles in the Greek of this passage, many of which end with σα?

The Greek of Mark 5:25–27 uses seven participles, most

of which in the English are translated as finite verbs. In reality, however, the Greek contains *only one main verb*, ἥψατο. This "touching" is significant since the identical verb is repeated in Mark 5:28, 30–31. Repetition is a tell-tale sign of emphasis. Why would Mark want to call special attention to the touch that took place between this unclean woman and Jesus?

This story of the bleeding woman (Mark 5:25–34) does not stand alone but is incorporated into a typical Markan "sandwich" with the healing narrative of a dead girl—a story that begins and concludes this unit in Mark's gospel (Mark 5:21–24, 35–43). Certainly the "interruption" of the bleeding woman in the middle of the Jairus story creates a lively tension whereby the audience wonders whether Jesus will get to the sick girl before she dies. Remarkably, this girl is twelve years old, having been born in the same year that the woman's bleeding problem began.

Christology is central to the story since Jesus amazingly raises the dead girl. When he gets to her, he reaches out and touches (κρατήσας) her dead body, just as the woman has touched Jesus. According to Old Testament ceremonial legislation, touching a bleeding (i.e., menstruating) woman or a corpse rendered a person unclean (Lev. 15:19–33; 22:4; Num. 19:11–22). But here, instead of Jesus becoming unclean, the victims are healed. Jesus' kingdom-actions fulfill the Old Testament ceremonial laws so that now Jesus the Messiah cleanses people.

By combining these two stories that speak of Jesus' touch, Mark intends to demonstrate that the ceremonial laws regarding contact with corpses and menstruating women are no longer applicable under the new covenant. The discovery of the main verb in Mark 5:25–27 brings to light the thematic concept in the narrative: only by touching Jesus are the unclean made clean. The ultimate message demonstrates that Jesus' touch is effective not only for healing ceremonial uncleanness but the spiritual disease of sin as well. Discovering the main verb and distinguishing it from the subordinate participles offers unexpected insights into the meaning of this text.

Dean Deppe

Ἀνέβη δὲ καὶ Ἰωσὴφ ἀπὸ τῆς Γαλιλαίας ... εἰς πόλιν Δαυὶδ ... ἀπογράψασθαι σὺν Μαριὰμ τῇ ἐμνηστευμένῃ αὐτῷ, οὔσῃ ἐγκύῳ.

Participles are important in the Greek language, and we need to pay attention to them—not only to the aspect of the participle (present, aorist, perfect) but also to the type of participle. They can tell us so much about what might be going on behind the text.

Luke 2:4–5 talks about Joseph's trip to Bethlehem. In the ancient world, only men had to be counted in a census—to enroll either for tax purposes or for military purposes. Mary accompanied Joseph on his trip. This part in the story contains two participles. The first one is ἐμνηστευμένῃ, translated "the one pledged to be married." This participle is preceded by the article, which makes it an attributive or adjectival participle. As such, it describes something about Mary, namely, that at the time she and Joseph went to Bethlehem, they were not married. That circumstance should strike us as highly unusual, because engaged people in the ancient world were never to be seen together without their parents. Yet Joseph and Mary travel together all the way to Bethlehem, a distance of ninety miles, as an engaged couple.

The second participle is οὔσῃ, which can be translated "being." This participle is not joined by καί to the first one, nor does it have its own article. It is therefore an adverbial or circumstantial participle, which denotes some adverbial idea, such as time, cause, concession, means, condition, or the like. Which of these adverbial nuances best applies can only be determined by the context. I suggest that only two seem possible here.

Cause: "because she was pregnant." It is possible that Joseph had said to Mary, "Your baby, the Messiah, the Son of David, is supposed to be born in Bethlehem, and since you are about ready to give birth, you need to accompany me to Bethlehem in order to fulfill the prophecy of Micah."

Concession: "although she was pregnant." Have you ever reflected on how Mary fared on the road to Bethlehem, walking six days (minimum) on dusty roads, over hills and through valleys, *being nine months pregnant*? If instead she jolted up and down on a donkey, her comfort level would have been no better. But why did she make that trip if she herself didn't have to be enrolled in the census? A concessive nuance to οὔσῃ may imply that Joseph was the only one who believed the story of Mary's pregnancy and that she had nowhere else to live. Joseph had, of course, been charged by God to take care of Mary (Matt. 1:20–21); was it possible that Mary, pregnant under suspicious circumstances, was no longer welcome to live with her parents? I think so. So *even though* Mary was nine months pregnant, when Joseph had to go to Bethlehem, she had to go along. And through that means, God saw to it that Micah 5:2 was fulfilled.

Verlyn D. Verbrugge

Whose Righteousness?

Εἶπεν δὲ καὶ πρός τινας τοὺς πεποιθότας ἐφ' ἑαυτοῖς ὅτι εἰσὶν δίκαιοι καὶ ἐξουθενοῦντας τοὺς λοιποὺς τὴν παραβολὴν ταύτην· Ἄνθρωποι δύο ἀνέβησαν εἰς τὸ ἱερὸν προσεύξασθαι, ὁ εἷς Φαρισαῖος καὶ ὁ ἕτερος τελώνης. ὁ Φαρισαῖος σταθεὶς πρὸς ἑαυτὸν ταῦτα προσηύχετο, Ὁ θεός, εὐχαριστῶ σοι ὅτι οὐκ εἰμὶ ὥσπερ οἱ λοιποὶ τῶν ἀνθρώπων, ἅρπαγες, ἄδικοι, μοιχοί, ἢ καὶ ὡς οὗτος ὁ τελώνης· νηστεύω δὶς τοῦ σαββάτου, ἀποδεκατῶ πάντα ὅσα κτῶμαι. ὁ δὲ τελώνης μακρόθεν ἑστὼς οὐκ ἤθελεν οὐδὲ τοὺς ὀφθαλμοὺς ἐπᾶραι εἰς τὸν οὐρανόν, ἀλλ' ἔτυπτεν τὸ στῆθος αὐτοῦ λέγων, Ὁ θεός, ἱλάσθητί μοι τῷ ἁμαρτωλῷ. λέγω ὑμῖν, κατέβη οὗτος δεδικαιωμένος εἰς τὸν οἶκον αὐτοῦ παρ' ἐκεῖνον· ὅτι πᾶς ὁ ὑψῶν ἑαυτὸν ταπεινωθήσεται, ὁ δὲ ταπεινῶν ἑαυτὸν ὑψωθήσεται.

In Luke 18:1–8 Jesus tells the story of the unjust judge and the persistent widow, a story in which he uses the δικ- word group six times (18:3 [2x], 5, 6, 7, 8). The widow asks for "justice" against her "adversary" (18:3). Although he is unlike God ("unjust"; 18:6), the judge nevertheless grants "justice" to the widow lest she wear him down (18:5). Jesus asserts that God will bring "justice" for his chosen ones (18:7–8) and concludes the story with an important question: "However, when the Son of Man comes, will he find faith on the earth?" (18:8). You can almost hear the religious leaders of Jesus' day answer the question, "Of course the Son of Man will find faith when he returns. We are the guardians of the faith. While others may fade away, we will remain faithful."

In the next episode, Jesus continues the emphasis on justice using the δικ- word group, though it is virtually impossible to see its three occurrences in an English translation. In the parable of the Pharisee and the tax collector in Luke 18:9–14, Jesus responds to an inappropriate kind of faith—one in which people (1) seek to establish their own righteousness (δίκαιοι) rather than receive God's righteousness and (2) look down on everyone else (18:9). Luke's use of δίκαιοι links the two stories.

Although "justice" and "righteousness" are from the same Greek word group, we English speakers usually fail to connect the concepts because, unlike the Greek, the words in our English translations do not share a common root. What's more, we can easily fail to see how both are central to an authentic faith (πίστιν in 18:8).

Jesus tells of two men who go to the same place (the temple) for prayer. The Pharisee, standing by himself (or perhaps praying silently), makes himself the *subject* of his prayer (using "I" four times) and boasts of religious accomplishments that set him apart from "this tax collector" (18:11–12). Hidden in the list is the Pharisee's denial that he is an "evildoer" (ἄδικοι in 18:11), the second occurrence of the δικ- word group. The second man, a tax collector, stands at a distance, unwilling to look up to heaven but beating his chest in grief and hoping to become the *object* of forgiveness: "God, have mercy on me, a sinner" (18:13).

The parable concludes as Jesus announces God's surprising verdict on the two men: "I tell you that this man, rather than the other, went home justified [δεδικαιωμένος] before God" (18:14a). The use of "this man" (οὗτος) to describe the repentant tax collector marks him as thematically central to the discourse. In addition, we see in this verse the third occurrence of the δικ- word group, this time to describe the tax collector's justification before God.

One man trusting in his own righteousness (δίκαιοι) left with only his self-justification. The repentant man, however, throwing himself on God's mercy, returned home a new man — δεδικαιωμένος before God.

Jesus concludes the story with two divine passives: "For all those who exalt themselves will be humbled [by God], and those who humble themselves will be exalted [by God]" (18:14b). Genuine faith, the kind Jesus will be looking for at his return, involves simple humility and dependence on the Lord in contrast to any sort of self-reliance. Little wonder that in the next story Jesus calls adults to embrace childlike faith if they want to enter the kingdom of God (18:15 – 17).

J. Scott Duvall

A Close-Up
Look at Forgiveness

Ὁ δὲ Ἰησοῦς ἔλεγεν, Πάτερ, ἄφες αὐτοῖς, οὐ γὰρ οἴδασιν τί ποιοῦσιν.

Taking notice of the aspect and *Aktionsart* of the verbs in the Passion Narrative can help the reader appreciate in a deeper way the drama of Jesus' death (Luke 23:32–49). Verbal aspect refers to the way in which verbs show the viewpoint or perspective of the author concerning an event. When the viewpoint is external, or seen from the outside, the aspect is perfective. When the viewpoint is internal, or seen from within the event as it unfolds, the aspect is imperfective. *Aktionsart* (a German word that means "type of action") gives much more specific information about the verb. It takes into consideration the context of how the verb is used and shows how the action takes place.

Now imagine the crucifixion of Jesus unfolding like scenes from an epic play on the stage of human history. The aorist verbs ἦλθον ("they came"), ἐσταύρωσαν ("they crucified"), ἔβαλον ("they cast [lots]"), and ἐνέπαιξαν ("they mocked") form the narrative backbone of the opening scene as the characters perform their respective parts (vv. 33–36). The perfective aspect of the aorist verbs offers an external viewpoint of the characters' actions, and we as readers see the scene of Jesus' death initially from a distance. Or, to use the metaphor of the camera lens, the perfective aspect offers the zoom-out or panoramic view of Calvary.

Then the stage director and master storyteller, Luke, zooms in on the cross of Jesus by using the imperfect verb ἔλεγεν (v. 34). The imperfective aspect of ἔλεγεν moves us into closer proximity of the cross. Time almost seems to slow down when we, along with the soldiers, the crowds, the religious rulers, and the two criminals on either side, hear Jesus say: "Father, forgive them, for they do not know what they are doing."

The interpreter might be tempted to see the *Aktionsart* or kind of action for ἔλεγεν as repetitive and translate ἔλεγεν as an iterative imperfect. We would then read ἔλεγεν to mean: "Jesus *kept on saying*, 'Father, forgive them....'" While the iterative imperfect is an exegetical possibility, it is better to translate ἔλεγεν as an instantaneous or dramatic imperfect. As a dramatic imperfect, ἔλεγεν is translated: "Jesus *said*." But it also means that *he said with intensity*, "Father, forgive them!..." The imperfect not only brings us the readers closer to the cross (aspect), but it also is used here to convey a vivid, emotion-laden, time-slowing declaration of forgiveness (*Aktionsart*). It makes for an awe-inspiring moment that stuns all onlookers. Drawn into the narrative ourselves, we realize that Jesus' prayer was not only for his executioners, but also for us, whose sins ultimately crucified Jesus rather than the actual nails (cf. Acts 2:36).

One of the two criminals who hung alongside Jesus was especially shaken by the prayer. This bandit confessed that as a sinner he was rightly being judged by God for what he had done (v. 41). He humbly said (ἔλεγεν): "Jesus, remember me when you come into your kingdom" (v. 42). The first ἔλεγεν (by Jesus; v. 34) inspired the second ἔλεγεν (by the criminal; v. 42). One dramatic imperfect is met with another. In other words, Jesus' prayer of forgiveness was answered by the bandit's own prayer of repentance. As the camera starts to zoom out and return to a panoramic view of Calvary, we are left with Jesus' promise: "I say to you, Amen!

Today you will be with me in paradise" (v. 43). This same offer of forgiveness is available to all who respond to Jesus not with the anger of the first bandit (v. 39) but with the brokenness, humility, and repentance of the second.

Max J. Lee

Πάντα δι᾽ αὐτοῦ ἐγένετο, καὶ χωρὶς αὐτοῦ ἐγένετο οὐδὲ ἕν ὃ γέγονεν.... ὁ νόμος διὰ Μωϋσέως ἐδόθη, ἡ χάρις καὶ ἡ ἀλήθεια διὰ Ἰησοῦ Χριστοῦ ἐγένετο.

The gospel of John begins with a prologue (common in ancient literature) that serves as the lens through which the rest of the gospel must be read. Prologues usually introduced the important characters, overall plot, and unseen forces at work in a story. What holds this prologue together and directs its message is the carefully crafted use of one Greek word group: that stemming from γίνομαι. It occurs in every section of the prologue, thus forming a sort of highway on which the message of this prologue travels. The root word itself is flexible in meaning and so is translated in various ways: "made," "came," "become/became," "the One and Only" (NIV). Its significance, however, is not only its repeated occurrence, but also its progressive development throughout the prologue.

Beginning in verse 3, the author uses γίνομαι emphatically three times to describe Jesus as the one who created all things, and uses it with different tenses to express both the completed act of creation (aorist) and its continuing effects (perfect). The idea of "creation" behind the use of γίνομαι in verse 3 depicts Jesus as central to all the creative work of God.

In verse 6 γίνομαι occurs again, though this time it describes the arrival of John the Baptist. While there is an intended contrast between John (the witness) and Jesus (the one witnessed to), the noticeable presence of γίνομαι in this verse implies that a related force is also at work here. John would not have used this verb four times in six verses without allowing the occurrences to work in a coordinated manner. Behind the witness of John is the God of creation (v. 3), now working within creation. The author could have used the imperfect "was" (ἦν), which would have described John the Baptist from the inside. Instead, he signals to the reader that even the ministry of the Baptist is subsumed under the creative working of God.

After being used again in verse 10 in a manner similar to that in verse 3, γίνομαι occurs in verse 12 for a sixth time to describe the "creative" force of God in forming "children of God." This transformation can only be described (with Paul) as a new creation (2 Cor. 5:17), thus connecting this use of γίνομαι with verse 3 regarding the creation of the world.

Verse 14 contains the seventh (a significant number) occurrence of γίνομαι, when John describes how the Word "became" flesh. This incarnation is the ultimate manifestation of God's "creative" activities. The God who had been working from the outside is now on the inside; the Creator is now with his creation. Verse 14 also describes Jesus with a new title adopted from the root of γίνομαι: "the One and Only" (repeated in v. 18). By means of this eighth use Jesus has become the pinnacle of creation, the center of human history and all created things. The ninth use of γίνομαι, in verse 15, reinforces Jesus' place in history and the plan of God.

Finally, in verse 17 γίνομαι occurs for a tenth (another significant number) time to describe how the gospel of Jesus Christ is the ultimate "creative" act of God. The same power God used to create the world is at work in the person and work of Jesus Christ. God's children — those who respond to the gospel — are born out of the same power that created the world. Through γίνομαι this prologue describes with progressive precision the important characters, overall plot, and unseen forces at work in the story of the gospel.

Edward W. Klink III

You and You

Ἀπεκρίθη Ἰησοῦς καὶ εἶπεν αὐτῷ, Ὅτι εἶπόν <u>σοι</u> ὅτι εἶδόν <u>σε</u> ὑποκάτω τῆς συκῆς πιστεύεις; μείζω τούτων ὄψῃ. καὶ λέγει αὐτῷ, Ἀμὴν ἀμὴν λέγω <u>ὑμῖν</u>, ὄψεσθε τὸν οὐρανὸν ἀνεῳγότα καὶ τοὺς ἀγγέλους τοῦ θεοῦ ἀναβαίνοντας καὶ καταβαίνοντας ἐπὶ τὸν υἱὸν τοῦ ἀνθρώπου.

One reason for the great popularity of the gospel of John consists in its portrayal of the personal, one-on-one contacts that Jesus develops with individual searchers. The climax of chapter 1 narrates Jesus' encounter with Nathaniel, who is overwhelmed by Jesus' personal knowledge of him while he sat "under the fig tree." But Jesus calls the attention to a spectacular future event when heaven itself will open and angels will ascend and descend on the Son of Man. From the flow of the narrative and the English translation, "You will see heaven opened," this future event appears to be particular to Nathaniel only. But the Greek reveals a subtle alteration from the second person singular to the second person plural:

> Jesus answered him, "Because I said to you [σοι], 'I saw you [σε] under the fig tree,' do you [sing.] believe? You [sing.] will see greater things than these." And he said to him, "Truly, truly, I say to you [ὑμῖν], you [pl.] will see heaven opened, and the angels of God ascending and descending on the Son of Man." (ESV)

As indicated by the change from singular to plural, Jesus' word is not just for Nathaniel but for all of Jesus' disciples as well.

Just as Jacob's Bethel experience (alluded to here) was not meant for Jacob alone, so Jesus' words to Nathaniel have a broader audience—all God's people.

The angels ascend and descend on Jesus at his resurrection when one heavenly messenger is positioned at the head and another at the feet where Jesus had lain (20:12). This symbolic portrait of two angels attending God/Jesus represents the ark of the covenant, where the divine presence rested among God's people to offer atonement and mercy to all. Jesus himself is God incarnate among us. The plural pronoun in 1:51 points to a reality in which every Christian can partake. All of us can now experience a ladder to heaven and enjoy real temple fellowship with the Son of God because of Jesus' resurrection.

A similar change in pronouns occurs in Jesus' conversation with Nicodemus in John 3. In 3:7 Jesus explains to Nicodemus, "You [σοι] should not be surprised at my saying, 'You [ὑμᾶς] must be born again.' " Even though this nighttime conversation is private, the fourth evangelist intends every reader to participate in this personal encounter with Jesus. All of us must be born again. Jesus' exhortation has universal significance.

This dialogue represents a conversation between unbelieving Jewish leaders in the first century and the Christian church, led by Jesus. Without realizing it, Nicodemus (a Pharisee; 3:1) speaks prophetically in the plural : "We know (οἴδαμεν) that you are a teacher who has come from God" (3:2). Then in 3:11 – 12, the dialogue displays the contrasting faith of Christians, on the one hand, and unbelieving Jews, on the other hand, when Jesus gives to Nicodemus personally (σοι [sing.]) a message for everyone. All the remaining occurrences of "you" in these verses are plural.

Once again, a change in Greek pronouns demonstrates that all of us must enter into a conversation with Jesus. As a result of such a personal encounter, "we speak of what we know, that we have received a heavenly revelation from Jesus to which we witness every day" (cf. 3:11). The pronouns allow us as readers not only to listen to a dialogue between Jesus and a single person, but also to enter into the narrative itself. Through the Scriptures we are transformed.

Dean Deppe

Jesus Gets Angry at Death

JOHN 11:38

Ἰησοῦς οὖν πάλιν ἐμβριμώμενος ἐν ἑαυτῷ ἔρχεται εἰς τὸ μνημεῖον.

If you have ever suffered deep pain such as the death of a loved one or a life-threatening illness, have you wondered how Jesus felt about your suffering?

Sometimes the Scriptures tell us how Jesus felt about things. In the story of the death of Lazarus in John 11, we read how Jesus felt about what sin and sickness and suffering and death were doing to the family he loved. By application, we also see how he feels about your brokenness and pain.

He's sad about it, right? Yes — the text says he wept (11:35). It's comforting that Jesus experiences our pain deeply. Yet he doesn't just feel sadness. There's something more!

Notice the Greek verb ἐμβριμάομαι that occurs in both 11:33 and 11:38. Many versions translate the term as "deeply moved" or something similar. Yet the use of the term elsewhere plus the immediate context points to a more likely word meaning in John 11.

In classical Greek this word is used of horses "snorting" as they prepare to charge the enemy in battle. In the Greek Old Testament, the term refers to "indignation" (Lam. 2:6) and rage (Dan. 11:30). Occasionally, the word is also used elsewhere in the Gospels:

- Mark 1:43: Jesus **"sternly warns"** a man not to report his healing.

- Mark 14:5: people **"rebuke"** or **"scold"** a woman for anointing Jesus with expensive perfume.
- Matthew 9:30: Jesus again **"sternly warns"** two blind men not to announce their healing.

The translation "deeply moved" falls short of capturing the emotional power of ἐμβριμάομαι. Rudolf Schnackenberg's conclusion is worth repeating: "The word *embrimasthai* ... indicates an outburst of anger, and any attempt to interpret it in terms of an internal emotional upset caused by grief, pain or sympathy is illegitimate." Only a couple of translations seem to get it right: "indignation" (NLT) and "angry" (HCSB).

As Jesus goes to the tomb of Lazarus, he isn't just overwhelmed with sadness and grief. He's also righteous with rage. He's fighting mad. He's angry at sin, suffering, disease, and most of all, death! He's furious at these evil powers for hurting the people he loves so deeply.

This interpretation of ἐμβριμάομαι as referring to righteous anger rather than emotional distress is supported by the commands that follow. Grief-stricken people don't normally start issuing strong commands.

- 11:39: "Take away the stone."
- 11:40: "Didn't I tell you that if you believed, you would see the glory of God?" (a question that here functions like a command).
- 11:43: "Lazarus, come out!"
- 11:44: "Take off the grave clothes and let him go!"

Martha was right. One day God will raise his children from the dead. Jesus is the resurrection! But Jesus is also the life, and the life starts here and now. You can trust Jesus right in the middle of all that you are suffering. Knowing how he feels about your suffering will strengthen your faith. The truth is that your suffering not only grieves Jesus, it also angers him deeply. He's mad at sin, sickness, disease, and death for hurting you, his precious child.

J. Scott Duvall

Taking Up the Cross

JOHN 13:4

Ἐγείρεται ἐκ τοῦ δείπνου καὶ τίθησιν τὰ ἱμάτια, καὶ λαβὼν
λέντιον διέζωσεν ἑαυτόν.

Jesus' call to his disciples in the Synoptic Gospels is clear. "Whoever wants to be my disciple must deny themselves and take up
their cross and follow me" (Matt 16:24). We are called to "take
up our crosses" and die to ourselves.

It is less clear exactly what Jesus means when he asks us to
"take up our cross." Are we to imitate him in his death by literally
dying on a cross, or literally dying on behalf of others? Are we all
called to go to a closed country and be physically persecuted for
Jesus' sake?

It is interesting that the gospel of John lacks this call to take
up one's cross. In fact, depending on the English version one uses,
it can be difficult to see in John's gospel anything at all that one is
to "take up," except for the healed paralytic's taking up his "mat"
(John 5:8). Reading the Greek text instead of relying on English
translations, however, presents a different picture. John 13:4 gives
us great insight into the meaning of "*taking up* the cross."

The English versions say that Jesus either "took off" or "laid
aside" his outer garment, and "wrapped," "girded," or "took" a
towel. If we read only the English translations, we would properly
conclude that Jesus' foot washing is the model par excellence of
what it means for us Christians to serve others with humility. Just
like Jesus, *we* are to take the role of the servant/slave and wash
others' feet.

48

If we stop there, however, we will miss a gold nugget. Let's translate this verse literally (note the words in italics): "And he rises from the supper and *laid down* [τίθημι] the garments, and *taking up* [λαμβάνω] a towel, he wrapped it around himself."

You don't have to be an expert in John's gospel to hear the "laid down–take up" chorus singing in your ears. These words in Greek are *exactly* the same as the words Jesus said a couple of chapters earlier: "The reason my Father loves me is that I *lay down* [τίθημι] my life—only to *take it up* [λαμβάνω] again. No one removes it from me, but I *lay it down* [τίθημι] of my own accord. I have authority to *lay it down* [τίθημι] and authority to *take it up* [λαμβάνω] again. This command I received from my Father" (John 10:17–18).

Jesus is talking about physical death in 10:17–18, but in 13:4 he applies those same terms to the *service* he expects of his followers. In other words, serving others is a type of death to self.

What does it mean to "take up the cross"? It means that we are to "lay down" our selfish desires by "taking up the towel" in order to serve others humbly and sacrificially! It does not necessarily mean that we must physically die, though it might mean doing so. But "taking up the cross" is much more mundane. It means serving our fellow humans in the midst of their dirt and grime: doing dishes for the family, coaching soccer in our communities, visiting the homeless and taking them a meal, helping the widow by mowing her lawn, listening to friends pour out their troubles, washing windows for an elderly couple. The options are endless—whatever selfless, sacrificial task a servant/slave might do. When we do these things—and this is the cool part—we die to ourselves. And *that*, in the gospel of John, is what it means to "take up [your] cross."

Matt Williams

Play on Words

JOHN 15:2–3

Πᾶν κλῆμα ἐν ἐμοὶ μὴ φέρον καρπόν, αἴρει αὐτό, καὶ πᾶν τὸ καρπὸν φέρον καθαίρει αὐτὸ ἵνα καρπὸν πλείονα φέρῃ. ἤδη ὑμεῖς καθαροί ἐστε διὰ τὸν λόγον ὃν λελάληκα ὑμῖν.

One of the most difficult tasks in translating the New Testament is rendering into English a play on words in the Greek text. When that play on words branches (pun intended) into metaphors and into the relationship between our salvation and a life of holiness, it moves from "difficult" to "almost impossible." Then add in John's use of double meanings and nuances, and many translators go screaming into the night.

I was once asked about the relationship between "prunes" and "clean" in John 15:2–3: "Every branch [κλῆμα] of mine that does not bear fruit he takes away [αἴρει], and every branch that does bear fruit he prunes [καθαίρει], that it may bear more fruit. Already you are clean [καθαροί] because of the word that I have spoken to you."

Several things are going on here. First, κλῆμα is not the normal word for "branch," which is κλάδος. Κλῆμα is more appropriate for the tendrils, the suckers that will never produce fruit and yet absorb life-giving nourishment. So the image is of the vinedresser removing anything that will take nourishment away from the fruit-bearing branches.

Life in the vine (i.e., Jesus) is intended only for those branches that can and will bear fruit. Branches able to bear fruit need to be pruned (καθαίρω) in order to bear more fruit. This verb can be used in a physical sense of pruning, but it can also mean "to clean," such as when you sweep a floor clean. Jesus is starting to shift from a physical truth to a spiritual truth. He is concerned with the spiritual cleanness and purity as well as the fruitfulness of his followers.

While the pruning process is not painful to an apple tree or a vine, it can be painful to Jesus' followers. Although we are to count all things in the context of joy, the snipping of God's shears can be painful, whether it means losing a job, or friends, or security, or personal goals. The question is: Is our pruner all-loving and all-knowing? The answer, of course, is "Yes."

As the disciples listened to Jesus and heard him talking about cutting off dead wood and pruning the new fruit on the vine, I suspect they were looking puzzled. (Perhaps most of the Upper Room Discourse puzzled them.) Jesus wants to assure them, now that Judas is gone, that they are not dead wood to be cut off and burned. They are true branches attached to the life-giving vine, Jesus. But that means the vinedresser will be snipping away at them. In fact, they have already been *pruned back*; they have already been *purified* by the message of the Messiah (feel the play on words).

These are wonderful words of encouragement to the disciples—despite all the ups and downs they have experienced and the big one that is yet to come (a crucified Messiah), they are firmly attached to the vine and have been prepared by God to bear much fruit. It has hurt, and it is going to hurt, but that does not mean the vinedresser doesn't know what he is doing. In fact, like the disciplining of a son, the pruning is part of their assurance that God knows exactly what he is doing, and the end of the process is their own spiritual growth and the glory given to God through our fruit.

William D. Mounce

Conditional Clauses Matter

ACTS 5:38–39

Καὶ τὰ νῦν λέγω ὑμῖν, ἀπόστητε ἀπὸ τῶν ἀνθρώπων τούτων καὶ ἄφετε αὐτούς· ὅτι ἐὰν ᾖ ἐξ ἀνθρώπων ἡ βουλὴ αὕτη ἢ τὸ ἔργον τοῦτο, καταλυθήσεται· εἰ δὲ ἐκ θεοῦ ἐστιν, οὐ δυνήσεσθε καταλῦσαι αὐτούς, μήποτε καὶ θεομάχοι εὑρεθῆτε.

The word "if" is a short one (in both Greek and English), but especially in Greek it packs great exegetical significance. Three examples, all in Luke-Acts, serve as illustrations. A first-class condition presents the situation as though it were so ("If, and for the sake of argument, let's say it is so..., then..."); such a condition uses εἰ in the "if" clause. A second-class condition is contrary to fact ("If, but such is not the case for the sake of argument..., then..."). This construction uses εἰ plus the imperfect tense in the "if" clause, followed by ἄν and an indicative in the "then" clause. A third-class condition makes no presentation either way ("If, and I am not saying which way it goes..., then..."). A third-class condition uses ἐάν; but most translations in English do not signal these differences, so you need to know Greek to notice them. Let's see how they work.

In Luke 7:39, Jesus has allowed a sinful woman to anoint him with tears and oil. The Pharisee who hosts Jesus sees this act and says: "If [εἰ] this man were [ἦν] a prophet, he would know [ἐγίνωσκεν ἄν] who and what kind of woman this is who is touching him, that she is a sinner." This sentence presents a second-class condition. To the Pharisee, Jesus must not be a prophet because he allows the act to take place. Then in delicious irony, Jesus tells the Pharisee a parable that indicates he knows exactly what the Pharisee is thinking and how skeptical he is. Score one for Jesus and Luke.

In Acts 5:38–39, Gamaliel uses two conditional clauses side by side. He is warning the Jewish leaders about taking action against Peter and John. He says, in effect, that if what they do is from men, the movement they are leading will fail. But if it is from God, they can do nothing to stop it. Here are the two clauses side by side: "So in this case I say to you, stay away from these men and leave them alone, because if [ἐάν] this plan or this undertaking originates with people, it will come to nothing; but if [εἰ] it is from God, you will be unable to stop them, or you may even be found fighting against God." The first conditional clause is third class, so it makes no commitment either way. However, the second conditional clause is a first-class condition, so it is presented as more likely than the first case.

Here Luke is playing with Gamaliel, because Gamaliel would have spoken in Aramaic or Hebrew, neither of which makes such fine distinctions as Greek makes in conditional clauses. In other words, Gamaliel likely presents the two options as equal. Luke, however, makes clear in his presentation that the second situation is more likely the case (as his entire book of Acts shows). Score another one for Luke. Just as we often say in my home state, "Don't mess with Texas," so here Gamaliel is warning the leaders not to mess with a movement that could be from God. Time will tell, he says.

And time has told, for the movement never did die. Luke uses conditional clauses to send a strong theological message about the permanence of the Christian movement.

Darrell L. Bock

Paul: Bound in the Spirit for Jerusalem

ACTS 20:22

Καὶ νῦν ἰδοὺ δεδεμένος ἐγὼ τῷ πνεύματι πορεύομαι εἰς Ἰερουσαλήμ

In 2004 my wife and I decided to relocate to Turkey. After a time of prayer and fasting, we felt that the Holy Spirit gave us the green light to move. As we shared our plans with friends and family, this decision was met with skepticism, even fear. In the post-9/11 environment they were concerned about what might happen to us in a Muslim country where Americans and Christians were presumed to be hated. While we thanked them for their concern, we felt compelled to follow the leading of the Holy Spirit regarding our relocation.

In Acts 20:22, Paul was at a critical phase of his public ministry toward the end of his third journey. Traveling with a group of eight companions including Luke, he was carrying the collection from Gentile believers to Christians in Jerusalem. At Miletus Paul summoned the Ephesian elders, and there he delivered the speech found in Acts 20:18–35. In the midst of his speech we find a verse that the NIV translates: "And now, compelled by the Spirit, I am going to Jerusalem" (v. 22); the NLT translates the first clause, "And now, as a captive to the Spirit...." Both the Louw and Nida and the Thayer lexicons suggest "compel" as a legitimate translation for δέω, thus giving a metaphorical sense to the verb.

The verb δέω in its literal sense continues as an important

catchword in Acts. In 21:11 the prophet Agabus came down from Jerusalem to Caesarea to meet Paul. Binding (δήσας) his own hands and feet with Paul's belt, he declared, "The Holy Spirit says, 'In this way the Jewish leaders in Jerusalem will bind [δήσουσιν] the owner of this belt and will hand him over to the Gentiles.'" This prophetic act coupled with a prophetic word confirmed what the Holy Spirit had spoken to Paul along the journey (see 20:23). At Tyre believers had urged Paul through the Spirit not to visit Jerusalem (21:4). Nevertheless, after Agabus's warning, the apostle reiterated his determination to continue: "I am ready not only to be bound [δεθῆναι], but also to die in Jerusalem" (21:13).

In Jerusalem Paul soon found himself in trouble with a crowd at the temple. The Roman commander arrested him and had him "bound" (δεθῆναι) with two chains (Acts 21:33). In his speech before the crowd Paul noted the irony of his situation. Some two decades before he was the one intending to bring "bound" (δεδεμένους) believers from Damascus to Jerusalem for punishment (22:5). As the Roman commander was interviewing Paul, he realized he had violated Roman law because he had "bound" (δεδεκώς) a Roman citizen (22:29). Later in Caesarea, Paul was "bound" (δεδεμένον) as a prisoner of the Roman governor Festus (24:27).

Somewhere along his journey, perhaps on the solitary walk to Assos (Acts 20:13–14), Paul had submitted himself to God's will for whatever lay ahead. Thus he was bound in the Spirit long before anyone bound him in Jerusalem and Caesarea. The guidance of the Holy Spirit is a pervasive theme throughout Acts, and it reminds us that we can never be successful in life or ministry without his direction.

Yes, my wife and I have encountered challenges living in a culture very different from our own. But, like Paul, we can look back and see how the Holy Spirit directed us to take that step. There is peace and comfort in knowing that it was God's Spirit who bound us in our task of advancing the kingdom even before we arrived in Turkey.

Mark W. Wilson

Kicking against the Goods

ACTS 26:14

Πάντων τε καταπεσόντων ἡμῶν εἰς τὴν γῆν ἤκουσα φωνὴν λέγουσαν πρός με τῇ Ἑβραΐδι διαλέκτῳ, Σαοὺλ Σαούλ, τί με διώκεις; σκληρόν σοι πρὸς κέντρα λακτίζειν.

Understanding the cultural background of the first century is often critical in learning to understand some of the idioms and imagery of the Greek New Testament. These idioms sometimes get lost in translation.

Take, for instance, the phrase from Acts 26:14, where, on the road to Damascus, the Lord Jesus says to Paul (at that time referred to as Saul): "It hurts you to kick against the goads." The NASB, NIV, ESV, and even the NRSV all use "goads." (The KJV uses "pricks" — not a good word to use today!) What are "goads" (κέντρα)? We do sometimes use the English expression: "You goaded me into it." Likely, however, most modern English-speaking persons do not know what a "goad" is.

The Greek term κέντρον (sing.) basically means a "sharp point," and it has negative connotations. The word is used in Revelation 9:10 to describe the locusts that arise from the Abyss when the fifth angel sounds his trumpet; these locusts have "stings [κέντρα] like scorpions." The same word occurs as a metaphor in 1 Corinthians 15:55–56 to refer to the "sting" of death (which Paul identifies as "sin").

Generally in Greek literature, a κέντρον is a pointy stick that functions similarly to a whip in controlling an animal. An animal's owner wanted to make sure the animal did what it had been purchased to do—such as plow a field or carry something to market. In other words, a κέντρον is analogous to the electric cattle prod that farmers use today. Obviously, for an animal to kick against a κέντρον would result in the animal's hurting itself. An ancient Greek proverb depicts a horse saying to a donkey, "Let him not keep kicking against the goads." Why not? Presumably because it was self-defeating behavior that resulted in pain and more pain.

In Jesus' message to Saul/Paul spoken from heaven, the reference to κέντρα was a metaphorical way of saying that as Saul was persecuting the church, he was actually hurting himself. Saul was sinning against God by resisting God's plan for his life. And the fact that Jesus uses a present tense infinitive in λακτίζειν ("to kick") suggests that as long as Saul is persecuting the church, he is continuing a self-defeating activity—he is hurting himself. True, at the time Saul was persecuting the church, he believed he was pursuing God's will by trying to stamp out the fledgling Christian movement. Later in life, however, he carried a burden of personal guilt over his "previous way of life in Judaism" (Gal. 1:13–14, 23; cf. also 1 Cor. 9:15–18; Phil. 3:6; 1 Tim. 1:12–15).

God's message to us is the same. The more we sin against God, the more we resist his plan for our lives, and the more we tune out his call into our lives, the more pain we will feel. Indeed, we are only hurting ourselves when we keep running into the brick wall of sin. Later on in life we may, like Paul, wonder whether God perhaps considers us the chief of sinners. But, as God showed his forgiving mercy to Paul, he will show his forgiving mercy to us if we repent of our sins, turn to Jesus Christ as Lord, and accept his will for our lives.

Ben Witherington III

Paul's (Often-Missed) Pointer to an Old Testament Text

Δικαιοσύνη γὰρ θεοῦ ἐν αὐτῷ ἀποκαλύπτεται ἐκ πίστεως εἰς πίστιν, καθὼς γέγραπται· ὁ δὲ δίκαιος ἐκ πίστεως ζήσεται.

Even though in Greek ἐκ is an incredibly common preposition and the noun πίστις (in its various forms) is also a common word, a search through ancient Greek literature, papyri, and inscriptions fails to turn up any examples of ἐκ πίστεως in extant Greek before Habakkuk 2:4 (LXX). Then in the New Testament books of Romans and Galatians it shows up twenty-one times (and once each in Hebrews and James). This expression would not have been a familiar construction to Paul's readers, except that they may have known it from Habakkuk 2:4. But Paul doesn't hesitate to use the expression over and over again (at least in those two letters), and more often than not in that same formulation.

In fact, Paul only uses ἐκ πίστεως in the two letters in which he also quotes from Habakkuk 2:4. In various passages Paul rewords the expression to provide some clarification of how he thinks it should be understood (using διὰ πίστεως [Rom. 3:22; Gal. 2:16; Phil. 3:9]; ἐν πίστει [Gal. 2:20]; or εἰς πάντας τοὺς πιστεύοντας [also Rom. 3:22]). In other words, whenever Paul uses ἐκ πίστεως, he is most likely echoing the text in which the expression first appeared and which provided him one of his keys to understanding justification by faith.

What the reader of Greek may notice, but others will not, is the range of texts in which that exact expression shows up in the Greek text but is translated differently in English translations. For example, in Romans 1:17, where Paul quotes Habakkuk 2:4, he uses ἐκ πίστεως twice—once in the quotation and once leading up to it. But while the expression as used in the quotation of Habakkuk 2:4 is almost always translated "by faith," its first occurrence in Romans 1:17 is virtually never translated that way, but rather as "from faith." My point is not that both occurrences should necessarily be translated in the same way, but rather that the reader of the Greek text should note a relationship invisible to someone who is only reading English translations.

In fact, in the first part of Romans 1:17, as Paul leads up to the quotation from Habakkuk 2:4, he provides his own interpretive rendering of Habakkuk's text (which seems to find fuller expression in Rom. 3:22). That interpretation consists in the idea that the righteousness of God revealed in the gospel (and testified to in the Law and the Prophets) comes to us through faith in (or "of") Jesus Christ; that is, God's righteousness is given "to all who believe" in him. In 3:22, εἰς πάντας τοὺς πιστεύοντας may well be an unpacking of what Paul meant by εἰς πίστιν when in 1:17 he placed it immediately after ἐκ πίστεως. In other words, righteousness ἐκ πίστεως is righteousness (given) to faith (εἰς πίστιν)—that is, given to all who believe (εἰς πάντας τοὺς πιστεύοντας).

This interpretation is certainly debatable. But my main point is that given the rarity of the expression ἐκ πίστεως in Greek prior to the New Testament and given its explicit association with (and grounding in) Habakkuk 2:4 in Paul's letters, those who read the New Testament in Greek would do well to note wherever the expression occurs and to consider whether Paul might be echoing this Old Testament verse (or his other teaching based on that verse). Such an approach may deepen one's understanding of Paul's teaching on faith.

Roy E. Ciampa

Peace with God

ROMANS 5:1

Δικαιωθέντες οὖν ἐκ πίστεως εἰρήνην ἔχομεν πρὸς τὸν θεὸν διὰ τοῦ κυρίου ἡμῶν Ἰησοῦ Χριστοῦ.

No one would dispute the pivotal importance of Romans within the theology of Paul. Throughout Christian history from Augustine to Calvin to Hans Urs von Balthasar, Romans has played a critical role in how we understand our faith. Romans may even be Paul's attempt to work out the theological intricacies of the chief doctrines he had been preaching since the start of his career. Here we find compelling descriptions of the condition of human life under God (sinful), the necessary and gracious intervention of God (through the life, death and resurrection of Christ), and the hope that is ours (justification and transformation).

Paul's argument reaches a key turning point in Romans 5. The apostle has already described God's indictment of humanity (1:8 – 2:29) and signaled that everyone — Jew and Gentile alike — share the same jeopardy: *All have sinned and fallen short of the glory of God* (3:23). Even among those who might claim some exception (Paul's imagined debating opponents in synagogues), Paul offers an unrelenting counterpoint: there are no exceptions. Jews are charged with being the custodians of the Scriptures (3:2), but it is those very Scriptures that record the jeopardy in which humanity finds itself. *Both Jews and Greeks are under the power of sin* (3:9). Paul then cites those Scriptures to show how mistaken people are (3:11 – 18). Inherent righteousness has eluded the life of every human being.

But in 3:21 Paul provides the solution. The righteousness unobtainable by us is available through God himself. The salvation we seek is not a salvation that comes from "below," as it were; it comes from "above" and is found only within the gracious intervention of God himself in Christ. His gracious gift resolves the crisis of human paralysis in sin.

Is this idea new? Not at all. The precedent is as old as Abraham (Rom. 4), and our participation in the faith of Abraham guarantees our access to this grace. Identity as one of God's people in Christ, therefore, is not based on ethnicity; Gentiles — sinners who share the same jeopardy as Jews — now also share the same access to the spiritual lineage of Abraham!

So now Paul writes: "Since we are justified by faith, we have peace with God through our Lord Jesus Christ" (5:1). The problem here is that "we have peace" appears in our Greek manuscripts in two forms, which would have sounded alike when read by scribes copying the manuscript. Some documents read ἔχομεν (present indicative), while others read ἔχωμεν (present subjunctive). The variation here is simply between two verbs with different forms of the "o" vowel: an omicron (the indicative) versus an omega (the subjunctive). Most Greek manuscripts attest the subjunctive, as do many of the Greek Fathers. However, most modern commentators follow the many scribes who here have added marginal corrections in their texts. The indicative is a statement of fact; the subjunctive implies a hope or something not quite realized.

The indicative is certainly Paul's meaning here. There is no doubt about our justification and peace with God. The apostle has just described the confidence with which we can now approach God (Rom. 3 – 4). From this fact, we can begin to explore the new life now available. Paul is no longer hoping that we might attain this peace — he knows that in Christ we *have* it.

So Paul's ringing affirmation must be primary in the translation ("we have peace"), and the participle must become subordinate ("having been justified"). Good news! Since we have been justified through the death of Christ, we possess peace with God *now*. It cannot be taken away.

Gary M. Burge

God and Human Tragedy

Οἴδαμεν δὲ ὅτι τοῖς ἀγαπῶσιν τὸν θεὸν πάντα συνεργεῖ εἰς ἀγαθόν, τοῖς κατὰ πρόθεσιν κλητοῖς οὖσιν.

The pastor was well-intentioned, but his comments didn't produce much comfort. "All things work together for good for them that love God," he had assured the grief-stricken mother whose son had just been killed by a drunk driver. Having memorized this verse in the King James Version as a girl, she knew Romans 8:28 by heart. But was it really true? Were Christians supposed to believe that an out-of-control vehicle driven by a reckless, irresponsible drunk was something that was working together for good? Besides, how could "things" — inanimate objects and events — that had no consciousness of their own "work together" for anything?

Linda talked with her good Christian friend Marlene about her questions. "You need to compare translations," she said. "The King James isn't always the most reliable option. I prefer to read the New American Standard Bible. For Romans 8:28, it reads, 'God causes all things to work together for good for those who love God.'" That satisfied Linda more. At least now it didn't sound like pantheism — like everything in the world is somehow brought about as part of one giant impersonal force. It seemed clear in this translation that God was in charge. But she still wasn't sure she believed God had *caused* this drunk driver to kill her boy. That didn't seem to mesh with the God of love she had been taught to trust.

After Marlene went home, Linda thought it was worth checking still more translations. Going to www.biblegateway. com, she noticed that the first translation to come up was the New International Version, which reads, "in all things God works for the good for those who love him." Now this she could accept. It didn't make God out to be the direct cause of the evil action but assured her that God was present even in the midst of those horrible circumstances, to bring something good out of the evil. She didn't yet know what that good would be, but over the years she had heard enough stories of people being saved or other amazing events transpiring after tragic accidents, sometimes as a direct result of those events. She hoped the NIV was the most accurate translation here, but she didn't know any Greek. She wished her pastor had taken Greek seriously in seminary, but he hadn't. On a couple of occasions she had met Dr. Smith, however, who taught Greek at the local Christian college. Maybe he'd be kind enough to offer an answer, so she emailed him her question.

He was happy to respond. He explained first that there is a textual variant in verse 28. Some manuscripts explicitly make God the subject of the verb "works together." Even if Paul did not originally write "God," he is clearly the implied subject from the context. "All things work together for good" is just not a helpful translation. But then there is a grammatical as well as a textual problem. "All things" (πάντα in Greek) is a neuter plural that could represent either the nominative or the accusative case. That is, πάντα could be either the subject or the direct object of "works together." But if "God" is the subject, then "all things" can't be the subject. Moreover συνεργεῖ ("works together") is an intransitive verb—it does not take an object. So what alternatives are left? The most likely answer is that πάντα represents an adverbial accusative meaning "in all things." The NIV *did* present the best translation, and it was also the one that made the most theological sense. Linda was grateful for Dr. Smith's insight and willingness to help.

Craig L. Blomberg

God Will Destroy Temple Destroyers?

1 CORINTHIANS 3:17A

Εἴ τις τὸν ναὸν τοῦ θεοῦ φθείρει, φθερεῖ τοῦτον ὁ θεός.

First Corinthians 3:17a has been called the most stringent warning in all of Paul's letters. The frightful prospect of God destroying someone who destroys his temple deserves closer scrutiny. First, the identity of ὁ ναὸς τοῦ θεοῦ (3:16–17) is crucial here. Does it refer to the individual believer, the universal church, or the local church? In verse 16, the sustained use of second person plural verbs (οἴδατε, ἐστε) and the plural pronoun (ὑμῖν) combined with the singular predicate nominative (ναός) favor a collective interpretation. The immediate context (3:5–15) further establishes that ὁ ναός refers to the local church in Corinth.

Second, since Paul threatens divine destruction for destroying God's church, we must identify the type of church destruction that is involved. Since Paul does not specify in the immediate context how the church is destroyed, the reader must consider the larger literary context (1:10–4:21). This section suggests the very behavior of the community prompted Paul's admonition on which his warning is predicated. The Corinthian community cultivated worldly wisdom (1:10–2:16), which resulted in jealousy, envy, strife, and division (3:1–4:21). The apostle confronts this mind-set by setting the message of the cross over against the world and its wisdom (1:18–25). Immediately following his warning in 3:17, he again focuses on the themes of "the wisdom of the world" and "boasting" (3:18–23).

Third, as to the target of Paul's warning, many argue that the prospective temple destroyer cannot be a true believer. However, at least three considerations weigh against this view. (1) Paul has been discussing the nature of Christian leadership within the church (3:5–15). He has not transitioned from teachers and believers to false teachers and unbelievers. While εἴ τις could certainly include unbelievers (i.e., false teachers or false professors), it is unlikely contextually that Paul is introducing a new audience here. The same expression is used in 3:12 in reference to Corinthian saints (or teachers). Paul provides no hint of a change in referent. The Corinthian saints are still under consideration. (2) The deliberate switch from third person singular (3:5–15) to second person plural (3:16–17) directly addresses the Corinthian saints. Again, no obvious contextual clues indicate that the warning against temple destroying relates to unbelievers. Instead, believers are being admonished. (3) Paul recognizes that true believers are susceptible to fleshly desires and behavior (e.g., 3:1–3; cf. Rom 13:14; Gal 5:16–26), as evidenced by the severe problems addressed in 1 Corinthians and elsewhere.

Finally, we must probe the meaning of φθείρω, which is used twice in 3:17. The repetition relates God's response directly to the offense. Paul places the initial use of φθείρω at the end of the protasis, and he fronts the second use at the beginning of the apodosis, so that the forms appear back to back. The juxtapositioning of the verbs implies a close connection between the two actions. In the first use of φθείρω Paul warns the Corinthian community, whose moral misconduct is destroying the church. The second use of φθείρω is God's righteous response to a prospective temple destroyer's offense against the church. So Paul is using φθείρω to emphasize the certainty of God's judgment on anyone who destroys his temple—the apodosis points to the certainty of God's judgment, not to its timing. The burden of proof rests on those who would read eternal destruction into the apodosis. It is more likely that the destruction God imposes is temporal in nature and may involve physical ruin (e.g., weakness, sickness, death, 11:30). Thus, 3:17 serves as a severe temporal warning to those who destroy their local church body through moral misconduct.

Keith Krell

The Way Some of Us Were

I CORINTHIANS 6:11

Καὶ ταῦτά τινες ἦτε ἀλλὰ ἀπελούσασθε, ἀλλὰ ἡγιάσθητε, ἀλλὰ ἐδικαιώθητε ἐν τῷ ὀνόματι τοῦ κυρίου Ἰησοῦ Χριστοῦ καὶ ἐν τῷ πνεύματι τοῦ θεοῦ ἡμῶν.

A theological insight is often obscured in translation. For instance, the HCSB translates the verse above: "Some of you *were like* this; but you *were washed*, you *were sanctified*, you *were justified* in the name of the Lord Jesus Christ and by the Spirit of our God." It is a good translation, but grammatical elaboration can intensify Paul's point.

The first verb in the verse, ἦτε, is the imperfect of εἰμί, while the final three verbs shift to aorist passive forms, ἀπελούσασθε, ἡγιάσθητε, and ἐδικαιώθητε. If the imperfect tense represents ongoing action in past time, then Paul is focusing on how a converted church member's lifestyle *used to be*—how it *was* carried out on a day-to-day basis. The antecedent of ταῦτα is a salacious vice list that earned Corinth its seedy reputation in the first century—evidently, a list of sins that some of the Corinthians still had not abandoned. Paul's use of τινες instead of πάντες undoubtedly raised some eyebrows in the group. This reference heightens the inclusio bracketing the list in verses 9–10, where Paul stresses twice that those whose lifestyles are marked by these kinds of behaviors "will not inherit the kingdom of God" because the poisonous deeds of darkness still prevail, and their lives were characterized more by ἐστέ rather than ἦτε.

Juxtaposed emphatically with ἦτε, the triple occurrence of ἀλλά joins each of the other verbs in verse 11 to ἦτε and signals divine intervention. Each of those verbs is an aorist passive — they are "divine passives," which demonstrate that God's power has decisively and effectively delivered a significant blessing to lives that had been destined for disaster. The Greek language does not require ἀλλά to be included before each verb in order to communicate a contrast. By doing just that, however, Paul heightens his hearers' awareness of how striking their deliverance is.

Being "washed," "sanctified," and "justified" are not synonyms, but they do indicate the rich aspects of salvation; each one of these verbs is grounded in the Godhead as Jesus, the Spirit, and the Father respectively. Referencing the Trinity draws attention to the potential unity of the Corinthians, but it also displays their present disunity. Such disunity clearly violates the desire Jesus had for his disciples to be one just as he and the Father are one (John 17:20–23). Maintaining this unity was a chief ingredient of being a viable witness in the world. Having not actualized the reality of their salvation, many of the Corinthians had hearts in the world and bodies in the church.

The Corinthian church was characterized more by arrogance, pride, and toleration of immorality than by the living evidence of transformed lives. All of these aberrations listed by Paul were symptomatic of their disunity. With his threefold employment of ἀλλά, Paul intends to jolt them back to repentance and lead them to correct thinking and behavior.

When we become Jesus' disciples, we can no longer function as a part of the world's design. We are certainly in it, but we are no longer of it. Coming to the point of alienation with the world as evidenced by our spiritual cleansing, by our being set apart by God, and by our being made right with God means that we may no longer live as we once did. The message today is the same: the church in the world lives out the gospel; the world in the church is a disaster.

Paul Jackson

Why Is the Body of Christ Important?

1 CORINTHIANS 12:7

Ἑκάστῳ δὲ δίδοται ἡ φανέρωσις τοῦ πνεύματος πρὸς τὸ συμφέρον.

Each Christian is given a manifestation of the Spirit πρὸς τὸ συμφέρον. Most translations translate this as "for the common good." However, τὸ συμφέρον itself simply means "good" or "beneficial." What justifies adding the word "common" or "corporate" to our translations?

In antiquity, what constituted the "good" or "beneficial" was a prominent topic in philosophical and rhetorical discussions and was usually spelled out. For example, Plutarch writes of benefit in reference to Aratus's "native city," τὸ τῆς αὐτοῦ πατρίδας συμφέρον ("the benefit of his native city," *Aratus* 24.4). Sometimes a Greek writer did reference the *common* good by adding the word "common," as when Dionysius of Halicarnassus states that the best counselor is the one who gives his views with an eye to "the common good" (τὸ κοινὸν συμφέρον, *Roman Antiquities* 10.51.3).

Paul is addressing a significant problem in the Corinthian church in his use of πρὸς τὸ συμφέρον. After he has cited the generally accepted premise that gifts have been given "for the good," he goes on to identify in the rest of the chapter that, for believers, this good must be seen as something beneficial *to the*

72

body of Christ. The Corinthians had an incorrect understanding of what is "good" because they were focused on their individual συμφέρον. We see their self-interested mind-set in various ways, such as in how they were divided over leaders (1:12), ate idol food sacrificed to idols even if doing so caused a fellow believer to stumble (8:1–13), and lacked love for one another (13:1–13). The Corinthians must first understand that the basic lesson inherent in a Christian understanding of συμφέρον is the corporate good, and they must overcome their focus on their individual self-interest. That is, the "beneficial" element must be understood in the context of their new existence in the Spirit as the one body of Christ (12:12–27). Because they are in Christ, they are to consider the corporate good of the body as primary instead of their individual good.

We often read 1 Corinthians 12 to learn how to appreciate our spiritual gift, and so we are comforted to read that even if we are "only" a "hand" or an "ear," we are still important. While this assurance is certainly valid, the problem with this perspective is that, as with the Corinthians, it reflects a self-focus — one that makes us feel good — rather than a focus on the whole church as it belongs to Christ. When we do not begin by valuing the good of the whole, our natural tendency is to read the passage for assurance that *we* are okay. Like the Corinthians, we must get beyond this self-focused mode to see the importance of the whole to which we now belong and make caring for the body of Christ what we value as mutually beneficial. Only then can we truly learn to care for our fellow believers in Christ, which is to care for Christ himself.

Do we have an abiding appreciation for the body of Christ? Are we aware of what an amazing responsibility and honor it is to be a part of Christ's body? Do we value our relationship with each another as much as Paul records in 12:26: "If one member suffers, all the members suffer with it; if one member is honored, all the members rejoice with it"? Do we focus on loving one another (ch. 13) and using our gifts to build up the body (14:12)? God calls us to understand the significance of our identity as the one body of our Lord and Savior and that what is "good" is what benefits the whole body.

Michelle Lee-Barnewall

All Things New

Ὥστε ἡμεῖς ἀπὸ τοῦ νῦν οὐδένα οἴδαμεν κατὰ σάρκα· εἰ καὶ ἐγνώκαμεν κατὰ σάρκα Χριστόν, ἀλλὰ νῦν οὐκέτι γινώσκομεν. ὥστε εἴ τις ἐν Χριστῷ, καινὴ κτίσις· τὰ ἀρχαῖα παρῆλθεν, ἰδοὺ γέγονεν καινά.

A notable experience can result in a whole new outlook on life. It did for the apostle Paul. To all outward appearances, Jesus of Nazareth was a messianic pretender who rightfully died a criminal's death. At least, to the innocent bystander that appeared to be the case. Then, on the road from Jerusalem to Damascus, Paul encountered the risen Christ, and that encounter led to an entirely new point of view.

Paul had been wrong in his assessment of Jesus. Jesus died a criminal's death, but the criminal in this case was everyone *except* Jesus. After reevaluating the evidence, Paul's considered conclusion was that "one [Jesus] died for all [everyone else]" (2 Cor. 5:14). Paul had initially come to the wrong conclusion because the standards he used were wrong. "Once," he says, "we knew Christ according to the flesh, but now we know him thus no longer" (2:16). Like many of us, Paul had judged people κατὰ σάρκα ("according to the flesh"), a favorite phrase that occurs some twenty times in his letters. While the term σάρξ ("flesh") can refer to what is human and physical, here it has to do with that which is worldly. To know someone κατὰ σάρκα is, therefore, to form an estimate of that person on the basis of society's standards.

It is all too easy to jump to conclusions about people on the basis of such standards as the clothes they wear, the size of their house, the kind of car they drive, the schools they attended, or the amount of money they make. Yet, ἐν Χριστῷ ("in Christ") such distinctions cease to exist. Paul, in fact, goes further and declares, "If anyone is in Christ, that person is a new creation; the old has gone, the new has come" (5:17). Καινή ("new") denotes what is fresh or newly made. The Greek phrase καινὴ κτίσις can mean either "there is a new creation" or a "new creature." The former has to do with the dawning of a new age, the latter with the creation of new life within. In this case, the latter perspective is more appropriate. While Paul typically uses κτίσις of creation in its entirety, the previous verses speak of a new estimate of people, not of things. In other words, one who is ἐν Χριστῷ ("in Christ") has "become a new person altogether" (Phillips).

Paul calls his former way of viewing things τὰ ἀρχαῖα ("the old" way). When used of things, as here, τὰ ἀρχαῖα means "old-fashioned," "antiquated," or "worn out." This old way of thinking about things, Paul says, "has come and gone" (παρῆλθεν). The aorist verb points to something that has passed out of existence. In its place "has come something entirely new" (γέγονεν καινά). Paul's pronouncement is prefaced by ἰδού ("Look!" NIV), a particle frequently used to capture the attention of the listener or reader. The word καινά ("new") denotes that which is qualitatively better as compared with what existed until now. A better way of looking at things "has come" (γέγονεν). The tense is perfect—a new set of standards and attitudes has come to stay so that someone "in Christ" is now to be assessed in a completely new light. New creation in Christ is the ultimate leveler: "There is no longer Jew or Gentile, slave or free, male and female. For you are all one in Christ Jesus" (Gal. 3:28 NLT).

Linda Belleville

χάρις
   → ὑμῖν
  καὶ
εἰρήνη
  ἀπὸ θεοῦ
      πατρὸς
       ἡμῶν   **A**
  καὶ
    κυρίου
    Ἰησοῦ Χριστοῦ

4   τοῦ δόντος → ἑαυτὸν   **B**
    ὑπὲρ τῶν ἁμαρτιῶν
      ἡμῶν
    ὅπως ἐξέληται → ἡμᾶς
     ἐκ τοῦ αἰῶνος
       τοῦ ἐνεστῶτος
       πονηροῦ

    κατὰ τὸ θέλημα   **A´**
     τοῦ θεοῦ
     καὶ
     πατρὸς
     ἡμῶν
5   ᾧ ἡ δόξα
      εἰς τοὺς αἰῶνας
      τῶν αἰώνων ἀμήν

Galatians may well be the earliest epistle Paul wrote and the first document written in the New Testament. If so, Galatians 1:3–5 is our first extant articulation of the gospel of Jesus Christ. Here Paul presents the significance of Christ's sacrifice in a way that is both poetic in style and profound in theology. Between two phrases about θεοῦ πατρὸς ἡμῶν, Paul positions the gospel of the κυρίου Ἰησοῦ Χριτοῦ (resulting in an A B A' pattern). He begins by using the aorist participle of δίδωμι along with the accusative reflexive pronoun (ἑαυτόν) to proclaim that Jesus is the one who gave up his own life. In the gospels, we read how Judas handed Jesus over out of greed, the Jewish leaders because of envy, and Pilate from a desire to please the mob. Ultimately, however, it was Jesus himself who surrendered his life out of love. He did so "over" our sins (i.e., as payment for them on our behalf; ὑπὲρ τῶν ἁμαρτιῶν ἡμῶν), for the sake of our freedom (ὅπως ἐξέληται ἡμᾶς), and according to God's will (κατὰ τὸ θέλψμα τοῦ θεοῦ).

The first of these three phrases, which Paul pens to modify τοῦ δόντος, says that Christ gave his life "as payment to cover the debt of *our sins*." As John Stott once wrote, before we can understand the cross as something done for us, we must first understand the cross as something done by us. Indeed, our sins made it necessary for Christ to give his life so that "he might liberate us from this present evil age." This second phrase explains the purpose for Christ's death. Although so many evangelistic presentations tend to focus on forgiveness of sins or on going to heaven when you die, it is striking that here Paul stresses *freedom*. Furthermore, rather than our being set free from an eternal hell, Paul emphasizes liberty from the bondage of *this present evil age*.

It is true, of course, that freedom now is evidence of forgiveness of sins in the past and confirmation of eternal life in God's kingdom in the future. Christian liberty, however, is the keynote that sounds here and echoes throughout the subsequent passages — freedom from legalism (chs. 3–4) and from sinful passions (chs. 5–6). While not neglecting the importance of forgiveness or one's eternal destination, therefore, perhaps we should once more underscore—in both our evangelism and our discipleship—that it was for freedom that Christ set us free (τῇ ἐλευθερίᾳ ἡμᾶς Χριστὸς ἠλευθέρωσεν; see Gal. 5:1).

The last qualifying phrase assures the reader that the work of the Son was done in accordance with the Father's will. Paul goes on to explain that God's plan from the beginning was, in the fullness of time, to justify Jews and Gentiles through this good news of Jesus Christ. Such a marvelous plan and such a gracious gospel compel Paul to proclaim glory to God. In other words, because Christ came to rescue us ἐκ τοῦ αἰῶνος τοῦ ἐνεστῶτος πονηροῦ, Paul cannot help but give God praise εἰς τοὺς αἰῶνας τῶν αἰώνων.

Take a moment to consider the implications of such liberty. Have you allowed the gospel to go beyond forgiveness of your sins to personal freedom from legalism and lust? How might your life and your church look different if you emphasized this facet of the gospel?

J. R. Dodson

God's Promise to Bless All Nations

Προϊδοῦσα δὲ ἡ γραφὴ ὅτι ἐκ πίστεως δικαιοῖ τὰ ἔθνη ὁ θεός, προευηγγελίσατο τῷ Ἀβραὰμ ὅτι ἐνευλογηθήσονται ἐν σοὶ πάντα τὰ ἔθνη.

It is certainly possible to be a good student of the Bible without knowing Hebrew and Greek. There are many wonderful tools available for English-only students. So what good is there in knowing the original languages in which the Bible was written? When asked that question, my answer is always the same: knowledge of Hebrew and Greek gets you one step closer to God's original revelation and so even closer to the word of God. Consider, for example, Galatians 3:8 in three popular English Bible versions:

- NIV: Scripture foresaw that God would justify the Gentiles by faith, and announced the gospel in advance to Abraham: "All nations will be blessed through you."
- HCSB: Now the Scripture foresaw that God would justify the Gentiles by faith and foretold the good news to Abraham, saying, "All the nations will be blessed in you."
- ESV: And the Scripture, foreseeing that God would justify the Gentiles by faith, preached the gospel beforehand to Abraham, saying, "In you shall all the nations be blessed."

Though all three of these translations are good and sound translations of the original Greek, all three of them also miss important insights that are evident to the student who knows Greek. First, the verb "justify" is δικαιόω, which is related to other Greek words such as δικαιοσύνη ("righteousness, justice") and δίκαιος ("righteous, just, right"). To "justify" means to pronounce or declare "righteous." It also means to satisfy God's righteousness. The essence of the gospel is that God is righteous, just, and perfect, and we are not. The only way to satisfy God's perfection is for God to declare us "righteous," based on the righteous and perfect Jesus Christ, who died on our behalf on the cross. Reading an English translation that uses the word "justify" can easily miss the gospel message communicated in the connection between the "righteousness of God" (Rom. 1:16), which judges us as sinners, and God's pronouncing of us as righteous ("justification") through the perfect life and sacrificial death of Christ.

But there is another important insight in this passage that is only obvious to those who can read Greek. Notice that the passage says Scripture foresaw that God would "justify the *Gentiles* by faith," and then Paul quotes Genesis 12:3: "All *nations* will be blessed through you." While the English reader would likely see some connection between the "Gentiles" and the "nations," in the Greek this connection is crystal clear, since the word for "Gentiles" and "nations" is the same in Greek (τὰ ἔθνη). Paul says that God justified τὰ ἔθνη just as he promised Abraham that all τὰ ἔθνη would be blessed through him.

The point, of course, is that God is always faithful to his covenantal promises. When Adam and Eve sinned, all humanity entered a fallen state. Yet God launched a rescue operation by calling Abraham from his land and his people and by creating from him a nation through whom all nations would be blessed. That was the good news "announced ... in advance" to him. Through that nation descended from Abraham came

God's answer to human sin: Jesus Christ, the Righteous One. Paul's missionary activities as apostle to the "Gentiles" (τὰ ἔθνη) is fulfilling God's promise to restore all creation to himself. And that is the good news (εὐαγγέλιον, "gospel") that is still being preached—good news indeed!

Mark Strauss

The σύν-Mirror of Christian Salvation and Christian Unity

EPHESIANS 2:19–22

Ἄρα οὖν οὐκέτι ἐστὲ ξένοι καὶ πάροικοι ἀλλὰ ἐστὲ συμπολῖται τῶν ἁγίων καὶ οἰκεῖοι τοῦ θεοῦ ... ἐν ᾧ πᾶσα οἰκοδομὴ συναρμολογουμένη αὔξει εἰς ναὸν ἅγιον ἐν κυρίῳ, ἐν ᾧ καὶ ὑμεῖς συνοικοδομεῖσθε εἰς κατοικητήριον τοῦ θεοῦ ἐν πνεύματι.

Ephesians 2 provides a profound statement of salvation by grace (2:1–10) and the unity that Jews and Gentiles enjoy in Christ (2:11–22), and it is a carefully structured unit. The two halves of the chapter display a mirrored structure. In 2:1–10, the three main movements of the passage are: (1) *problem*: sin to the core of our being (2:1–3); (2) *solution*: made alive in Christ (2:4–7); (3) *consequence*: new creation (2:8–10). The same movements, but with different content, are seen in 2:11–22: (1) *problem*: disjunction between Jew and Gentile (2:11–12); (2) *solution*: Christ is our peace (2:13–18); (3) *consequence*: God's new household (2:19–22). The parallels between these two halves of Ephesians 2 demonstrate that Christ is the solution to sin and death, and he is therefore the solution to the disjunction between Jew and Gentile.

What is not so easily seen in English translation is that the parallels between the two halves of the chapter do not end there.

At the heart of the first half of Ephesians 2 are three Greek words prefixed by the preposition σύν: συνεζωοποίησεν, συνήγειρεν, and συνεκάθισεν. Believers have been *made alive with* Christ (2:5), been *raised with* him, and are now *seated with* him in the heavenly realms (2:6). Clearly, these σύν-prefixed words are significant for understanding a key theme of Ephesians—that of believers' union with Christ. But these σύν-prefixed words are also mirrored in the second half of the chapter. In 2:19–22, we read that Jews and Gentiles in Christ are now *fellow citizens*—συμπολῖται (2:19); are *joined together* in Christ—συναρμολογουμένη (2:21); and are *built together* for God's dwelling in the Spirit—συνοικοδομεῖσθε (2:22).

Is it merely coincidence that both halves of the chapter each have three closely spaced σύν-prefixed words, apparently in parallel? I think not. I believe that these two sets of σύν-prefixed words are deliberately mirrored and reflect a profound theological reality. Part of the logic between the two halves of the chapter is that because we are saved by grace and not by works, law, or ethnic heritage, Jew and Gentile alike are now on the same footing before God in Christ. All people that on earth do dwell may belong to the citizenship of God's household through Christ. And a central part of unity derives from a salvation by grace in which believers are made alive, raised, and seated *with* Christ. In other words, a consequence of our being *with* Christ is that Jews and Gentiles are now *with* each other. They are fellow citizens of God's household; they are joined together in Christ; and they are built together for God's dwelling in the Spirit.

Truly, our union with Christ brings about our union with each other. And as we see in Ephesians 2, a small Greek preposition helps us to appreciate that wonderful reality.

Constantine R. Campbell

Being Filled with the Spirit

EPHESIANS 5:18–22

Καὶ μὴ μεθύσκεσθε οἴνῳ, ἐν ᾧ ἐστιν ἀσωτία, ἀλλὰ πληροῦσθε ἐν πνεύματι, λαλοῦντες ἑαυτοῖς ἐν ψαλμοῖς καὶ ὕμνοις καὶ ᾠδαῖς πνευματικαῖς, ᾄδοντες καὶ ψάλλοντες τῇ καρδίᾳ ὑμῶν τῷ κυρίῳ, εὐχαριστοῦντες πάντοτε ὑπὲρ πάντων ἐν ὀνόματι τοῦ κυρίου ἡμῶν Ἰησοῦ Χριστοῦ τῷ θεῷ καὶ πατρί, ὑποτασσόμενοι ἀλλήλοις ἐν φόβῳ Χριστοῦ. Αἱ γυναῖκες τοῖς ἰδίοις ἀνδράσιν ὡς τῷ κυρίῳ.

Greek writers love the participle, and to master the New Testament one must master the participle. This passage has five participles: λαλοῦντες, ᾄδοντες, ψάλλοντες, εὐχαριστοῦντες, and ὑποτασσόμενοι, all of which function adverbially. That is, they modify the main verb in the sentence, which is the imperative πληροῦσθε ("Be filled!") in verse 18. Adverbial participles indicate the circumstances under which the action of the main verb takes place. But can we identify more closely in what way these five adverbial participles modify πληροῦσθε?

Greek grammars usually provide us with eight different nuances for the adverbial participle: they can indicate time, manner, means, cause, condition, concession, purpose, or result. Which of these functions applies depends on the context. Some interpreters have suggested *manner* here, so that the participles are describing the manner (the how) of being filled with the Spirit. Others have suggested *means*—describing actions to be performed in order to receive the filling of the Spirit. Dan Wallace argues that they are participles of *result*. That is, the actions of the participles are the result of being filled by the Spirit. He finds this most consistent with Paul's theology; moreover, these are present tense participles that follow the main verb.

Part of the difficulty in establishing the function is that adverbial participles are "undetermined" or "unmarked" for these kinds of nuances. That is, there are no words such as ὅτι, ἵνα, ὥστε, ὅτε, εἰ, ὥς, etc., to introduce the participles. Their sense depends on context. But we are not left entirely clueless, for the order of participles in relationship to the verb they modify is important. *When present tense participles follow the verb they modify*, they tend to explain and define that verb further. That is, they describe what is entailed in the action of the controlling verb.

Here in Ephesians 5:18–21, the five participles are *present tense* participles that *follow* πληροῦσθε; thus, they describe more clearly what it means to be filled with the Spirit. That is, being filled with the Spirit means to speak to one another in psalms and hymns, it means to sing and praise in one's heart, it means to give thanks, and finally it means to submit to one another in the fear of Christ. Whether these actions are more specifically the manner, the means, the purpose, or the result of being filled with the Spirit is not the most important issue. What is important is that they explain and define the verb πληροῦσθε. If we are to choose a specific nuance, that choice must be argued on the basis of the broader theological understanding of the work of the Holy Spirit in Paul and the New Testament as a whole.

In Ephesians 5:18–21 Paul calls for the church as God's temple to be filled with God's Holy Spirit (see 2:19–22); then, with a series of participles, he identifies what filling with the Holy Spirit looks like. God's people will participate in uplifting, corporate worship (speaking, singing, praying, giving thanks; vv. 19–20); furthermore, their relationships in the church and in the home will be transformed (submitting to one another; v. 21). Failure to participate in corporate worship or to demonstrate loving and serving relationships in our churches and homes surely means that we have not yet taken seriously this command to be filled with the Spirit!

David L. Mathewson

Γινώσκειν δὲ ὑμᾶς βούλομαι, ἀδελφοί, ὅτι τὰ κατ᾽ ἐμὲ μᾶλλον εἰς προκοπὴν τοῦ εὐαγγελίου ἐλήλυθεν.

To draw connections, sometimes biblical authors use the same word in different phrases. Such connections are lost when translations use, as they often must, different English expressions. Take Paul's use of μᾶλλον in Philippians. He boldly opens the body of this letter with these words: "I want you to know, brothers and sisters, that what has happened to me has actually [μᾶλλον] served to advance the gospel" (NIV). This translation denotes μᾶλλον as a term of certainty. The NASB translates the adverb in a more comparative manner: "for the *greater progress* of the gospel." What we easily miss is that Paul's use of μᾶλλον in 1:12 and elsewhere in his letter (1:9; 2:12, 23; 3:4) underscores an important spiritual truth, namely, that God can use what society considers shameful to achieve kingdom purposes in and through his people.

When Paul and his companion Silas first visited Philippi, the city authorities flogged them and threw them into prison — treatment that would have caused great shame to the victim's family and friends. During that night, an earthquake shook off the prinsoners' chains, and Paul then led the jailer and his whole household to know Jesus Christ (Acts 16:32–34). Upon Paul's release from prison, he returned to Lydia's house and encouraged the believers. Paul's imprisonment, in other words, furthered the gospel and strengthened the church.

Years later, Paul, again in prison (cf. "chains" in 1:14), writes to the Christians in Philippi and rejoices in his circumstances. His imprisonment, symbolized by chains, has made Christ known among the elite guard of the empire and has emboldened other ministers to proclaim the gospel fearlessly (1:12–18). Once again, Paul wants the believers to know that what society perceives as a loss of honor (his imprisonment), God has used as an avenue for reaching the lost and strengthening believers. All this is to say that Paul intentionally chooses the word μᾶλλον in 1:12 to accent the degree to which the gospel has advanced because of the things that have happened *to him* and *within* him.

Paul continues this section (1:19–26) by describing how he will in no way be ashamed but will boldly proclaim Christ, and that whether by life or death, Christ will be made great *in* him (1:20). Death will mean gain—to be with Christ is "by far better" (πολλῷ μᾶλλον κρεῖσσον, 1:23). But to continue living will mean Christ—believers will advance (1:25) in their knowledge about Christ. In Paul's initial thanksgiving section, this spiritual growth is, in fact, his prayer, namely, that the Philippians' love will "abound more and more [μᾶλλον καὶ μᾶλλον] in knowledge and depth of insight" (1:9).

In chapter 2, Paul stresses that he is not responsible for the Philippians' growth in knowing Christ. After describing Christ's humility—his shameful death on the cross—and his exaltation (2:6–11), Paul encourages the believers to let God work within them not only when he, the apostle, is with them, but "much more" (πολλῷ μᾶλλον, 2:12) when he is not. Later, Paul explains that while he has "more" reason (μᾶλλον, 3:4) to boast in his heritage and training, he considers them "loss" compared to knowing Christ. For Paul, what society considers honorable, he sees as a deficit; and what society perceives as shameful, God can use to advance the gospel.

Paul's thematic use of μᾶλλον, which is easy to miss in a translation, challenges us to change our societal lens for determining value. Pray for insight into how God might use the shameful circumstances in your life to bring about the knowledge of his Son in and through you. Be confident that Christ will continue to use events in your life to bring about the knowledge of him in others, more and more.

David Wallace

The Complete Work of Christ

PHILIPPIANS 2:5

Τοῦτο φρονεῖτε ἐν ὑμῖν ὃ καὶ ἐν Χριστῷ Ἰησοῦ.

One of the most beautiful passages in the New Testament is Philippians 2:6–11, commonly referred to as the Christ hymn, in which Christ's incarnation, work of salvation, and exaltation are presented with compelling force and in a poetic economy of words. The chapter's opening five verses set the stage for the hymn, but since 2:5 is elliptical, scholars have debated whether Paul cites the hymn primarily for doctrinal or for ethical purposes.

To evaluate the claims in the debate, an overview of 2:1–4 is important. Here we find highlighted both ethical and doctrinal concerns. On the surface, it is clear that Paul's interest is unity within the Philippian congregation. Yet his language in 2:1 calls to mind the Trinity, with its stress on Christ, love (of the Father), and the Spirit.

Paul uses the verb φρονέω ("think") twice in 2:2 and once in 2:5. Overall, he uses this verb ten times in Philippians — the most in any of his letters. Often, English translations render the verb as "having a mind-set" or "being of one mind." While these options convey the general sense of the term, they are technically inaccurate in that they obscure the fact that Paul chooses a verb, not a noun. This verb focuses on the action of processing thoughts and emotions or the task of forming careful judgments and discerning opinions.

That Paul uses a verb rather than a noun becomes especially important in interpreting 2:5, which can be translated literally, "this think among yourselves which also in Christ Jesus." Generally speaking, the reader inserts the verb of the first clause ("think") into the second clause. A second option is to use the verb "to be" in the second clause. Complicating matters is the direct object of the verb φρονέω — τοῦτο ("this"), which begins the sentence. Does this demonstrative pronoun look back to the previous four verses, or does it set the stage for the upcoming hymn? The resolution of one riddle affects the explanation for the other.

One interpretation of 2:5 emphasizes the ethical dimensions of the entire passage. The verb "to be" is added in the second clause, so that φρονέω in the first clause is calling for an attitude of humility among Philippian believers that mirrors Christ's own humility. The translation might be rendered, "Let this mind-set be in you that was in Christ Jesus." Paul charges each believer (and the church as a whole) to model their interactions and attitudes on the Exemplar, Christ, described in 2:6–11. The relative pronoun that begins the second clause (ὅ) is then (misleadingly) understood to refer to "mind-set," as though the antecedent of the pronoun were an implied noun: "this" (τοῦτο) is the antecedent of ὅ ("which").

A second solution stresses the doctrinal elements of the passage. The verb φρονέω is added in the second clause of 2:5, and the phrases "among you [pl.]" and "in Christ" are seen as parallel expressions of the believers' lives in the body of Christ: "Think this way [as explained in the previous verses] among yourselves as you also think in [your fellowship with] Christ Jesus." Seen this way, the verse urges the Philippian community to consider, with singleness of purpose, their lives together in the light of their relationship in Christ, who in addition to his salvation has also granted them the power for unity.

This second option has the advantage of highlighting the unique and complete work of Christ, the foundation on which rest all godly thoughts and obedient actions. By emphasizing the fullness of the incarnation and the surety of Christ's exaltation, Paul reminds believers that their unity, humility, and love are defined and empowered by Christ, for the Father's glory.

Lynn H. Cohick

One-Upmanship

Ἀλλὰ ἅτινα ἦν μοι κέρδη, ταῦτα ἥγημαι διὰ τὸν Χριστὸν ζημίαν. ἀλλὰ μενοῦνγε καὶ ἡγοῦμαι πάντα ζημίαν εἶναι διὰ τὸ ὑπερέχον τῆς γνώσεως Χριστοῦ Ἰησοῦ τοῦ κυρίου μου, δι' ὃν τὰ πάντα ἐζημιώθην, καὶ ἡγοῦμαι σκύβαλα ἵνα Χριστὸν κερδήσω.

I have three boys who constantly try to one-up each other. For instance, the other day, my ten-year-old son stated that he wanted to be a worship leader when he grew up. Not to be outdone by his brother, my seven-year-old said, "O yeah, when I grow up, I am going to be a pastor." My four-year-old settled the competition once and for all, however, when he proclaimed, "O yeah, when I grow up, I'm going to be God!" (Don't worry—we are working on his theology.)

In Philippians 3:2–6, Paul engages in a much more significant battle of one-upmanship. In a ferocious response to the boasts of his opponents—those "dogs," those mutilators of the members of men!—Paul decides to join in the "my confidence in the flesh is bigger than your confidence in the flesh" contest. Besides the *cutting* insults in verse 2, the apostle goes on to shame the prideful even more by laying down his own "boast" cards one by one: a seemingly royal flush. In our selected passage, however, Paul settles the score once and for all by turning the entire litany of boasts on its head. All these privileges, the whole of his achievements, the very status symbols Paul's opponents considered so much "gain," the apostle poignantly declares to be "loss" — completely worthless on account of Christ. They may pride themselves in their flesh, but Paul boasts in Christ. They may play cards of boasting, but Christ trumps them all.

If such a statement is not piercing enough to his opponents, Paul raises the bar twice more. Rather than just "those things" (ἅτινα) in his list, he now counts "*all* things" (πάντα) to be loss; indeed, he even regards them to be σκύβαλα (plural of σκύβαλον, "dung, excrement, manure, refuse, rubbish"). The apostle makes two more noteworthy points to reinforce his resolve. In verse 7, he uses the perfect tense (ἥγημαι) and then he switches to the present tense (ἡγοῦμαι) in verse 8. It is as though Paul is saying, "Not only have I regarded (with abiding results) these things as loss, but I continue to regard all things as loss." Further, the apostle's use of μενοῦνγε with ἀλλά and καί underscores the contrast all the more — "but truly indeed!"

To be sure, Paul does not discount these things because they are all inherently valueless (cf. Rom. 9:4–5; 11:1); rather he does so because of Christ, in order that he may gain Christ. All things (even a high GPA or a successful job) become worthless when compared to the surpassing worth of knowing Jesus Christ; therefore, to borrow from C. S. Lewis, he who has Christ and everything else has no more than he who has Christ alone.

Take a moment to make your own list. What privileges, talents, and accomplishments do you have that one might consider gain — national pedigree, family background, academic ability, financial stability, popularity, publications, service projects, communication skills, leadership positions, athletic prowess and achievements, trophies and awards, musical gifts, and physical beauty? Which of these "treasures" do you value most? How do these "most valuables" compare to your desire to know Christ? Do you find your identity, your confidence, more in them or in Christ? Pray that these "things of earth will grow strangely dim in the light of [Christ's] glory and grace."

J. R. Dodson

Conformed to Christ

PHILIPPIANS 3:20–21

ἡμῶν γὰρ τὸ πολίτευμα ἐν οὐρανοῖς ὑπάρχει, ἐξ οὗ καὶ σωτῆρα ἀπεκδεχόμεθα κύριον Ἰησοῦν Χριστόν, ὃς μετασχηματίσει τὸ σῶμα τῆς ταπεινώσεως ἡμῶν σύμμορφον τῷ σώματι τῆς δόξης αὐτοῦ κατὰ τὴν ἐνέργειαν τοῦ δύνασθαι αὐτὸν καὶ ὑποτάξαι αὐτῷ τὰ πάντα.

The Greek text of Philippians 3:20–21 offers two insights not readily apparent in a translation. First, the term πολίτευμα has two distinct properties not obvious in the text. (1) This word is better translated "commonwealth" or "state" because the emphasis is on the governing of the group. The closely related term πολιτεία refers to the constitution that establishes and defines the government. Polybius uses πολίτευμα for both government and constitution. (2) Today many countries automatically confer citizenship at birth on people born within their boundaries. But in Paul's day, citizenship was a rare privilege awarded by a particular city, such as Antioch or Alexandria. Yet both then and now, "citizenship" and "commonwealth" imply acceptance by a government. A citizen or commonwealth is defined in part by its government and its governing principles or tenets. Paul's point is that Christians are granted the supreme privilege of being members of the commonwealth of God, under the constitution of the gospel and led by the Savior, Jesus Christ.

In 1:27, Paul used the cognate verb πολιτεύομαι to encourage the Philippian believers to conduct themselves in the manner of any good citizen. We would expect Paul to use περιπατέω ("walk, walk around") or ζάω ("live"); but it is no accident that Paul uses πολιτεύομαι, since Philippi was a Roman colony, governed as though the city were located in Italy. Just as the citizens of Philippi (many of them Roman veterans) comported themselves with the pride and demeanor suitable to their social rank, so Paul urges believers to demonstrate by thought and deed their status as resident aliens under God's kingdom reign.

A second insight is the passage's close verbal connection to the Christ hymn in 2:6–11. These similarities explain the believer's redemption gained in Christ; three are worth highlighting. (1) The verb μετασχηματίζω ("transfigure, transform") shares the same root as the noun in 2:7, σχῆμα ("form, appearance"). The connecting thread is embodiment, as in 2:7 Paul highlights Christ's birth as a human (ἄνθρωπος), and in 3:21 a Christian's own body (σῶμα), which will be made suitable for eternal life established at Christ's return.

(2) The verb in 2:8, ταπεινόω ("make level, low"; metaphorically, "humble") is found in 3:21 in its nominal form, ταπείνωσις. In its literal sense, the noun describes a lessening, such as the reduction of swelling. Its metaphorical meaning, "humiliation, abasement," connotes both a moral sense and a social status. Paul explains Christ's death as humbling. (Interestingly, he does not say that Christ's incarnation was humbling.) He distinguishes the believer's present body as the body of our humiliation, perhaps because it is suffering and decaying and like Christ's body will also die. Paul may also evoke the word's connotation of status, for the Philippian believers were impoverished and persecuted. They stood on the bottom rungs of the social ladder and so appeared worthless. Paul declares that the opposite is true—they await the One who will subject all things unto himself (3:21).

(3) The hymn emphasizes that Christ, though in the form (μορφή) of God, took the form (μορφή) of a slave. In 3:21, Paul insists that believers' earthly bodies will be σύμμορφον

("conformed") to Christ's glorified body when he appears. Paul contrasts those whose minds are focused on earthly things (3:19) with the glorious age already inaugurated in Christ and to be consummated when he returns. The false cheers of "Caesar is Lord" and the worldly taunts against the Philippian believers will be silenced when Christ comes and puts all things right.

Lynn H. Cohick

Faith, Love...and Hope

COLOSSIANS 1:3-5

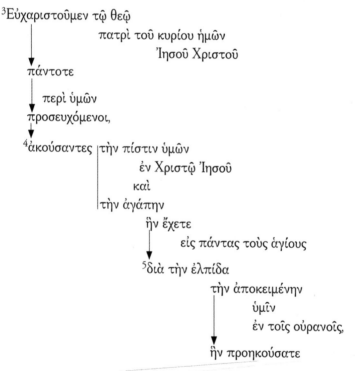

³Εὐχαριστοῦμεν τῷ θεῷ
               πατρὶ τοῦ κυρίου ἡμῶν
                      Ἰησοῦ Χριστοῦ
πάντοτε

  περὶ ὑμῶν
προσευχόμενοι,
⁴ἀκούσαντες | τὴν πίστιν ὑμῶν
                 ἐν Χριστῷ Ἰησοῦ
                 καὶ
       | τὴν ἀγάπην
            ἣν ἔχετε
                εἰς πάντας τοὺς ἁγίους
         ⁵διὰ τὴν ἐλπίδα
                τὴν ἀποκειμένην
                    ὑμῖν
                    ἐν τοῖς οὐρανοῖς,
             ἣν προηκούσατε
      ἐν τῷ λόγῳ τῆς ἀληθείας = τοῦ εὐαγγελίου

The opening lines in Paul's letter to the Colossians are ripe with exegetical insights drawn from the Greek text. In the first part of v. 3, the two appositional constructions (θεῷ = πατρὶ and τοῦ κυρίου = Ἰησοῦ Χριστοῦ) deepen our understanding and τοῦ κυρίου = Ἰησοῦ Χριστοῦ) deepen our understanding of both God (our Father) and the Son (Jesus Christ is Lord). We learn more about the nature of Paul's prayers for his fellow believers because of the adverb and two participles that modify εὐχαριστοῦμεν. He thanks God for them *when* he prays for them (προσευχόμενοι has a temporal nuance). Sometimes we can fall into the rut of thinking that when we pray, the only type of prayer that counts is intercession (the apostle gets there in vv. 9 – 14). Paul's example tells us that the times when thanksgiving rises in your spirit and spills out in conversation with God are deeply spiritual times of prayer.

Verse 4 gives the reason for Paul's thanksgiving in the adverbial participle ἀκούσαντες (a causal participle) — he thanks God *because* he has heard of their faith and love (parallel accusatives of direct object). When we hear of other believers following Jesus closely, thanksgiving becomes a language of celebrating their devotion. We also see both a vertical and horizontal dimension to the Christian life as the Colossians' faith is directed toward the Lord and their love toward fellow believers.

In the last part of v. 5 we have an example of the canon of Apollonius, named after the second-century Greek grammarian Apollonius Dyscolus. The rule simply says that both the head noun and the genitive noun(s) will either both have the article (articular) or both lack it (anarthrous): ἐν τῷ λόγῳ τῆς ἀληθείας τοῦ εὐαγγελίου. The last genitive (εὐαγγελίου) is an epexegetical genitive, meaning here that the word or message of truth is the good news or gospel.

Perhaps the most stunning exegetical insight is found in the interplay between the familiar triad of faith, hope, and love (cf. Rom 5:1 – 5; 1 Cor 13:13; Gal 5:5 – 6; Eph 4:1 – 6; 1 Thess 1:3; 5:8; 2 Thess 2:13). In some ways, these three words sum up the whole of the Christian life. But we know from love chapter (1 Corinthians 13) that ultimately love outranks the other two. Note too that in Colossians 1 πίστιν and ἀγάπην are parallel, with hope following in a prepositional phrase, διὰ τὴν ἐλπίδα, which provides the ground or the cause of faith and love. Did you catch that? Our faith and love are based on and dependent on hope.

Here hope refers to the content of the Colossians' hope since it is already reserved for them in heaven and since they heard about this hope previously when they heard the message of truth, the gospel. The same is true for us. Hope can rejuvenate our faith and love. Our hope of Christ returning to raise us from the dead, of God judging the forces of evil and restoring his creation, of the death of death, of life in God's wonderful presence with people who love him and love each other—this hope can show us why we should keep on trusting God and keep on loving people. While love might outrank hope, we sure need hope now to stay faithful and loving. Or to put the saying in different words: where there is hope, there is life (and faith and love).

J. Scott Duvall

Christ, Your Life

COLOSSIANS 3:4

Ὅταν ὁ Χριστὸς φανερωθῇ, ἡ ζωὴ ὑμῶν, τότε καὶ ὑμεῖς σὺν αὐτῷ φανερωθήσεσθε ἐν δόξῃ.

Most Christians like to describe themselves as having a relationship with Christ. We rightly say that we are interested not in a mere set of religious beliefs and practices but in a relationship with Jesus. In Colossians, Paul emphasizes this truth by his sevenfold repetition of σύν, meaning "with Christ."

<u>συν</u>ταφέντες αὐτῷ ἐν τῷ βαπτισμῷ	having been buried <u>with</u> him in baptism (2:12)
<u>συν</u>ηγέρθητε	you were raised up with [him] (2:12)
<u>συν</u>εζωοποίησεν ὑμᾶς <u>σὺν</u> αὐτῷ	he made you alive with him (2:13)
εἰ ἀπεθάνετε <u>σὺν</u> Χριστῷ	If you died with Christ (2:20)
εἰ οὖν <u>συν</u>ηγέρθητε τῷ Χριστῷ	If then you were raised up with Christ (3:1)
ἡ ζωὴ ὑμῶν κέκρυπται <u>σὺν</u> τῷ Χριστῷ	your life is hidden with Christ (3:3)
ὑμεῖς <u>σὺν</u> αὐτῷ φανερωθήσεσθε ἐν δόξῃ	you will be revealed with him in glory (3:4)

These claims suggest that "relationship" may not be a strong enough term! In some mysterious fashion, every believer in Christ is united with Christ, so that his death is ours, his burial is ours, his new life is ours, his position in heaven is ours, and his glorious return is ours. This closeness is what theologians refer to as "union with Christ," a central idea in Paul's teaching. Paul elsewhere clarifies this idea of union with Christ by comparing it to the union between spouses: "For it says, 'The two will become one flesh.' But the one who is united to the Lord is one spirit [with him]" (1 Cor. 6:16b–17). When I married my wife, my assets and debts became hers, and hers became mine. When we become "one spirit" with Christ, our debts are transferred to him, and his assets are transferred to us.

The "with Christ" claims in Colossians are amazing enough, but Paul uses an appositional phrase in 3:4 to take them a step further. "When Christ, your life, is revealed ..." (ὅταν ὁ Χριστὸς φανερωθῇ, ἡ ζωὴ ὑμῶν). An appositional phrase makes the second element ("your life") equal to the first element ("Christ"). In English, apposition is communicated by setting apart the second element with commas. In Greek, apposition is communicated by putting the second element in the same case as the first. Paul uses apposition at least a dozen times in Colossians: "Paul, apostle of Jesus Christ" (1:1); "we have redemption, the forgiveness of sins" (1:14); "God's mystery, Christ" (2:2). In every case, the second element describes the first. Just as Paul *is* an apostle and God's mystery *is* Christ, so Christ *is* our real life.

Christ is my real life! That may not be catchy enough to make a Christian bumper sticker, but it is a powerful truth with powerful implications. Paul gives us two of those implications in Colossians. First, our connection with Christ gives us *immeasurable security*. The Colossians feared the invisible, supernatural world; such fears are quickly dispelled when we realize that we are united with the one by whom "all things were created, in heaven or on earth, visible or invisible" (1:16). Second, our connection with Christ provides us with *genuine spirituality*. Like us, the Colossians were tempted toward various counterfeit forms of spirituality (2:8–21). Genuine spirituality is based on the amazing truth that we are deeply connected to Christ. By virtue of our union with Christ, we can lay aside the old self with its vices (3:8–10) and put on the virtues of Christ, the peace of Christ, and the word of Christ (3:12–16).

Gary Manning Jr.

Quench or Extinguish: What Are We *Not* Supposed to do to the Spirit?

I THESSALONIANS 5:19–20

Τὸ πνεῦμα μὴ σβέννυτε, προφητείας μὴ ἐξουθενεῖτε.

One of my favorite diversions is to sit around a crackling campfire on a cool evening, warm my hands over the fire, and watch the sparks disappearing into the darkness. Once the embers have died down, I'll roast some marshmallows and maybe even make a few sticky s'mores with graham crackers and chocolate bars. Finally, before going to bed, I'll douse the glowing coals with water to ensure the fire is out.

The 1984 NIV favors the literal interpretation of σβέννυμι in 1 Thessalonians 5:9: "Do not put out the Spirit's fire." To "extinguish" or "put out" is, in fact, the predominant meaning for the word in both the Septuagint and the New Testament. For example, Hezekiah faulted Judah because the priest had "put out the lamps" in the temple (2 Chron. 29:7). And Paul wrote that the purpose of the shield of faith is to "extinguish [σβέσαι] all the flaming arrows of the evil one" (Eph. 6:16).

First Thessalonians 5:19 is the only verse in the Bible in which the Spirit is the direct object of σβέννυμι. A literal understanding suggests that Paul is worried that the Thessalonians might extinguish or put out the Spirit in their lives. If that were the proper interpretation, the apostle would have envisioned a group close to falling away from the faith. However, even a cursory reading of this pericope shows that the Thessalonians, while in need of some exhortation, are not in danger of putting out the Spirit. These exhortations in verses 16–22 consist of eight commands in the imperative mood: six are positive with verses 19–20 conveying the only negative ones.

The majority of translations (including the NIV 2011) translate σβέννυμι figuratively by using the gloss "quench." Again there is a precedent for this approach in the Septuagint. Song of Songs 8:7 opines that "many waters cannot quench love." A cognate verb κατασβέννυμι in 4 Maccabees 16:4 portrays a devout mother who had "quenched" her many great emotions. BDAG suggest "stifle" and "suppress" as alternative English translations for this figurative meaning.

One challenge in using "quench" today is that the word typically brings to mind a commercial for some soft drink—a tanned surfer with his blonde girlfriend is refreshed by downing a particular brand of thirst-quenching soda. Even in John 7:37–39, Jesus compares the Spirit to a stream of living water that will quench the spiritual thirst of all who drink. However, in 1 Thessalonians it is those who have already drunk of the Spirit who are warned not to "stifle" him.

The second negative command in the passage may provide a clue for what stifling the Spirit might mean. In verse 20 the Thessalonians are commanded not to despise prophecies. Since in the New Testament the Holy Spirit is always viewed as the source of prophecy, to despise prophecy would be to hold in contempt the source of the prophecy. Indeed, if prophecy were despised, it would naturally be suppressed (stifled) in the public meetings. Thus the figurative meaning of σβέννυμι seems better to suit the context of the passage.

But how is the Spirit quenched or stifled today? Certainly churches and denominations adopt policies and practices that sometimes suppress the Spirit's activity. In our personal lives we can become so busy that living in the Spirit is stifled. Family and work responsibilities, answering email, keeping up with social networks such as Facebook — they all conspire daily to quench the presence of the Spirit. Thus Paul's admonition is still appropriate for us: "Don't put a lid on the Spirit" (my paraphrase).

Mark W. Wilson

A Celebration of God's Glory

2 THESSALONIANS 1:11–12

εἰς ὃ καὶ προσευχόμεθα πάντοτε περὶ ὑμῶν, ἵνα ὑμᾶς ἀξιώσῃ τῆς κλήσεως ὁ θεὸς ἡμῶν καὶ πληρώσῃ πᾶσαν εὐδοκίαν ἀγαθωσύνης καὶ ἔργον πίστεως ἐν δυνάμει, ὅπως ἐνδοξασθῇ τὸ ὄνομα τοῦ κυρίου ἡμῶν Ἰησοῦ ἐν ὑμῖν, καὶ ὑμεῖς ἐν αὐτῷ, κατὰ τὴν χάριν τοῦ θεοῦ ἡμῶν καὶ κυρίου Ἰησοῦ Χριστοῦ.

The overarching theme of 2 Thessalonians is the return of Christ. Chapter 1 describes Christ's return to judge his enemies, while much of chapter 2 outlines some of the events that precede that coming. Chapter 3 discusses the issue of the idle busybodies in Thessalonica, who probably stopped working because of their view of the immanence of Christ's return.

What comes to your mind when you think of the return of Christ? Heart-stopping fear? Excitement? Radiant joy? There is one word that is uppermost in Paul's mind when he writes about this amazing event: glory! In three short chapters, the apostle has five references to the glory of God, a percentage that is rivaled only by the Gospel of John.

- 1:9: God's enemies "will be ... shut out from the presence of the Lord and from the glory [δόξης] of his might."
- 1:10: "... on the day when he comes to be glorified [ἐνδοξασθῆναι] in his holy people."

- 1:12: "We pray this so that the name of our Lord Jesus may be glorified [ἐνδοξασθῇ] in you."
- 2:14: "... that you might share in the glory [δόξης] of our Lord Jesus Christ."
- 3:1: "pray for us that the message of the Lord may spread rapidly and be honored [δοξάζηται], just as it was with you."

Note also that the two uses of the verb ἐνδοξάζομαι are the only occurrences of this verb in the New Testament.

It is impossible not to think of the word "glory" when we think of heaven, where God is totally present. The pictures of heaven offered in Revelation 4–5, 21–22 are stunning and make even the most "glorious" sunrise or sunset fade into insignificance. And the most amazing thing is that we will some day "share in [this] glory" (2:14).

But God's glory is not simply something that describes the aura that presently surrounds God's throne (cf. 1:9), which we will observe and even bask in; it is something that we must reflect in our lives. That is the meaning of the verb unique to 2 Thessalonians: ἐνδοξάζομαι (to "in-glorify"). At the time of the return of Jesus Christ, he will be "glorified in [ἐν] his holy people" (1:10). When Jesus returns, in other words, the same glory that he manifests now as the holy Son of God will be obvious in his purified people.

But that reality should start becoming apparent right now. Paul's fervent prayer in 1:12 is that when people see us as followers of the Lord Jesus Christ, they will see the presence of the Lord of glory within (ἐν) us. Note that in both uses of the verb ἐνδοξάζομαι, the preposition ἐν is repeated for emphasis. This verb challenges us to live in such a way that people see the glorious Jesus reflected in our lives (see 2 Cor 3:18 for more on this). I am convinced that in this messy world people long to see those who stand out because they are living a life of caring for and sharing with others, just as Jesus gave his life for us.

Verlyn D. Verbrugge

Investments for Abundant Life

1 TIMOTHY 6:17–19

Τοῖς πλουσίοις ἐν τῷ νῦν αἰῶνι παράγγελλε μὴ ὑψηλοφρονεῖν μηδὲ ἠλπικέναι ἐπὶ πλούτου ἀδηλότητι, ἀλλ᾽ ἐπὶ θεῷ τῷ παρέχοντι ἡμῖν πάντα πλουσίως εἰς ἀπόλαυσιν, ἀγαθοεργεῖν, πλουτεῖν ἐν ἔργοις καλοῖς, εὐμεταδότους εἶναι, κοινωνικούς, ἀποθησαυρίζοντας ἑαυτοῖς θεμέλιον καλὸν εἰς τὸ μέλλον, ἵνα ἐπιλάβωνται τῆς ὄντως ζωῆς.

Paul's final charge to his protégé Timothy pertains to instructing well-to-do members of the Ephesian church. This instruction comes in the form of a military command: "Order [παράγγελλε] the rich in the things of this world." Normally, Paul "urges" (παρακαλέω) rather than gives orders. Possessions are not easily relinquished, however, and the desire for wealth can so easily consume us that nothing less than a command will do.

Paul does not denounce wealth per se, however; rather, he affirms that the world's goods are a gift from God, who "richly provides us with everything for our enjoyment" (v. 17b). The present-tense substantive participle τῷ παρέχοντι emphasizes that God is a giver who keeps on giving. Εἰς ἀπόλαυσιν does not have to do with spiritual enjoyment but instead with material pleasures. "The earth is the LORD's and everything in it" (Ps. 24:1). God takes pleasure in what he has created, and he intends that we do so as well.

With creation's riches, however, comes great responsibility. Those of us entrusted with the world's wealth have a threefold duty. (1) We must to use our wealth ἀγαθοεργεῖν (lit., "to be do-gooders"; v. 18). The Greek term denotes what is intrinsically good: as the Father is good, so we as his children are called to do good. This good-doing includes not just what we do for others but also what we do for creation God made us in his image to function as creation's caretakers (Gen 1:27–28), so doing good includes environmental responsibility. (2) We are to "be rich in good deeds" (πλουτεῖν ἐν ἔργοις καλοῖς, v. 18). The Greek word καλός denotes what is outwardly attractive; our "deeds" are to be eye-catching. (3) Finally, we must be "generous and always willing to share with those in need" (v. 18). The Greek term κοινωνικός means to hold in common, not in the sense of pooling congregational assets but instead in readiness to share. It requires an attitude different from a "me, myself, and I" perspective. Our possessions are gifts given to serve others as needs arise.

Paul notes two temptations to which the affluent are particularly prone. First, we can become proud and think highly of ourselves (ὑψηλοφρονεῖν). Our educational system encourages self-esteem—assuming that worldly success is our doing. Paul encourages God-esteem—viewing all that we are and have (πάντα) as "God's provision" (v. 17). The other temptation is to place our trust in what we possess (v. 17). The Greek perfect tense points to a settled opinion (ἠλπικέναι): "I am secure because I am well-off." Yet, such trust is misplaced, for wealth can be lost in the blink of an eye, as recent natural disasters and fiscal events in the global economy have shown.

Above all, we must rely on our spiritual investments. In our giving, Paul says, we "store up treasure as a good foundation for the future" (v. 19). Paul's advice previews the financial page of the *New York Times*. Our spiritual investments produce (ἀποθησαυρίζοντας is causative) a "good foundation" (θεμέλιον καλόν). The idea is that financial giving stores up spiritual wealth, which in turn pays secure dividends for the future (see Matt. 6:19–24). The dividends received are "experiencing true life" (v. 19). A Scrooge-like mentality may facilitate our continued earthly existence, but it does not lead to life as God intended—abundant, eternal life.

Linda Belleville

Guarding the Deposit
2 TIMOTHY 1:12B

οἶδα γὰρ ᾧ πεπίστευκα, καὶ πέπεισμαι ὅτι δυνατός ἐστιν τὴν παραθήκην μου φυλάξαι εἰς ἐκείνην τὴν ἡμέραν.

In the Pastoral Epistles, the apostle Paul encourages Timothy and Titus and gives them instructions on how to lead their respective churches. This approach in itself represents a significant change in Paul's modus operandi. For example, while living in Ephesus, Paul had tried his best to lead the church in Corinth by sending to it letters carried by trusted emissaries. But Paul became increasingly frustrated, especially as the "super-apostles" infiltrated the Corinthian church and sought to take over its leadership. So Paul began to place personal, on-site leaders in his churches — leaders such as Timothy in Ephesus and Titus in Crete. Paul expected them to lead these churches based on his instruction in letters written to them, not to the churches.

In 2 Timothy, Paul recites his own testimony of faith to encourage Timothy: "For I know whom I have believed, and I am persuaded that he is able to keep τὴν παραθήκην μου unto that day." The phrase I have left in Greek (lit., "my deposit, trust") is ambiguous as to whether μου represents a subjective or an objective genitive — that is, "what I have entrusted [to God]" or "what [God] has entrusted to me" (see NRSV note).

Dan Wallace in his grammar gives some strict parameters for dealing with subjective and objective genitives. The main (or head) noun must be a "verbal noun" — that is, a noun that is based on a verb. Παραθήκη is indeed a verbal noun, derived from παρατίθημι, a verb that can mean "to set something before someone, to set forth in teaching, to entrust for safekeeping." The following genitival noun (or pronoun) can then denote "what I have deposited somewhere for safekeeping" (subjective genitive) or "what has been deposited with me for safekeeping" (objective genitive). If the first meaning is Paul's intention, the noun παραθήκη would probably indicate Paul's entire life and ministry, which he has dedicated to God. If the second is his intention, the noun would probably denote the word of God with its teachings, which God has deposited with Paul and with every believer.

So, do we flip a coin to see which one we like best? No. The word παραθήκη occurs twice more in the Pastorals, and in both cases no genitive is added. In 1 Timothy 6:20, Paul instructs his young protégé to guard "the deposit [παραθήκη] by turning away from godless and empty talk and contradictions of what is falsely called knowledge." In 2 Timothy 1:14, Paul instructs Timothy forthrightly to "guard the good thing entrusted [παραθήκη] through the Holy Spirit dwelling in us." Essentially, both of these verses instruct Timothy to handle rightly God's word of truth entrusted to him (cf. 2 Tim. 2:15); in other words, only the objective genitive really fits Paul's message to Timothy in 2 Timothy 1:12b.

Rightly handling God's word of truth should be the goal of every student of Scripture: to study it faithfully and to preach/ teach it soundly. Doing so characterized Paul's own life (2 Tim. 1:12), and the Holy Spirit aided him. Moreover, God himself will see to it that his word and its message do not return to him empty. You can bank on that!

Verlyn D. Verbrugge

All Scripture

Πᾶσα γραφὴ θεόπνευστος καὶ ὠφέλιμος πρὸς διδασκαλίαν, πρὸς ἐλεγμόν, πρὸς ἐπανόρθωσιν, πρὸς παιδείαν τὴν ἐν δικαιοσύνῃ.

Second Timothy 3:16 is undoubtedly one of the most important statements made about the inspiration of Scripture—a statement made by the Bible about itself. To appreciate the significance of this verse, I offer five comments that address its grammar, context, meaning, extent, and application.

First, while there continues to be much debate regarding the translation of 2 Timothy 3:16, the grammatical possibilities reduce to only two main options. (1) We could translate the verse this way: "All Scripture is God-breathed and is profitable for teaching, for reproof, for correction, for training in righteousness...." This rendering argues that θεόπνευστος is a predicate adjective, which, by nature, restates the noun (γραφή) and requires the verb "is" between the two. On this reading, πᾶσα before a singular noun—in this case a technical noun and therefore not requiring the article—is correctly translated as "all" and the καί is copulative. All Scripture is inspired or God-breathed and therefore is profitable for holiness and Christian maturity.

(2) Others, however, argue that θεόπνευστος is an attributive adjective and thus precedes the noun, so that the phrase should be translated, "God-breathed Scripture." On this rendering πᾶσα should be translated "every" and καί as adjunctive. Thus, "every

God-breathed Scripture is also profitable...." Some interpreters balk at this latter option. They fear the resulting translation implies that not every word of Scripture is God-breathed and that only those words that are deemed inspired are profitable. But the context of this verse—the subject of my next point—rules out this nuance.

Verse 15 provides the immediate context of verse 16, and together they form parallel statements. Thus, if we chose option 2, we can translate verses 15–16: "... the sacred writings ... are able to provide you salvation through faith in Christ Jesus. Every God-breathed Scripture is also profitable for ... righteousness." The sacred writings in which Timothy was instructed were undoubtedly what we now know as the Old Testament. (The New Testament was still being written.) By placing these statements in parallel, Paul is equating "the sacred writings" (v. 15) and the "God-breathed Scripture" (v. 16); in other words, the entire Bible is inspired and therefore is profitable. This contextual consideration, therefore, suggests that regardless of one's grammatical choice for verse 16, the end result is the same.

Third, 2 Timothy 3:16 means that the divine origin of Scripture makes it useful for producing spiritual maturity in the believer's life. This truth is what Pastor Timothy needs to know and practice, and so also do Christian leaders today.

Fourth, as to extent of the "sacred writings ... Scripture," undoubtedly the Old Testament must be included. But by this time most of Paul's letters had been written, and in 2 Peter 3:15–16 Peter acknowledges they are part of the γραφή (same word) of God. Moreover, the words of Jesus were viewed as authoritative as well (see, e.g., 1 Cor. 11:23–26).

Fifth, the application of 2 Timothy 3:16 to the preaching of the word of God today is powerful. Since the entirety of the Bible is God-breathed, we ministers ought to declare the whole counsel of God, not just a portion of it. This spiritual principle will deliver us both from obsessing over one biblical author or over one biblical topic (such as eschatology or divine election), and will enable us to cover systematically every major portion of the Bible, even in an expository fashion. In so doing we will build up God's people in holiness and in maturity.

C. Marvin Pate

What Makes You Tick?

Ἐπεφάνη γὰρ ἡ χάρις τοῦ θεοῦ σωτήριος πᾶσιν ἀνθρώποις,
παιδεύουσα ἡμᾶς ἵνα ἀρνησάμενοι τὴν ἀσέβειαν καὶ τὰς κοσμικὰς
ἐπιθυμίας σωφρόνως καὶ δικαίως καὶ εὐσεβῶς ζήσωμεν ἐν τῷ νῦν
αἰῶνι, προσδεχόμενοι τὴν μακαρίαν ἐλπίδα καὶ ἐπιφάνειαν τῆς
δόξης τοῦ μεγάλου θεοῦ καὶ σωτῆρος ἡμῶν Ἰησοῦ Χριστοῦ, ὃς
ἔδωκεν ἑαυτὸν ὑπὲρ ἡμῶν ἵνα λυτρώσηται ἡμᾶς ἀπὸ πάσης ἀνομίας
καὶ καθαρίσῃ ἑαυτῷ λαὸν περιούσιον, ζηλωτὴν καλῶν ἔργων.

When I observe some extraordinary person, I often ask the question, "What makes him or her tick?" Recently, while sitting in a coffee shop, I had the chance to observe a woman from our church, and this question came to my mind. This woman had endured a lot of suffering over several years, yet here she sat discipling a younger woman. They prayed together and read from the Bible. They exchanged laughter, hugs, and tears. This extraordinary woman displayed compassion and confidence; she was filled with grace.

Grace—that's what made her tick. What makes you tick?

In Titus 2:11–14, Paul describes a life overwhelmed by God's grace. Grace becomes operative as it brings salvation and teaches us to live for Christ. Paul is anxious to see the initial role grace plays in salvation continue to influence the Christ-follower's everyday conduct. Grace, from start to finish, is what makes a true disciple tick.

Everything begins with God's initiating grace. The predicate adjective σωτήριος (notice it has no article and hence is predicative) modifies ἡ χάρις. This term expresses the idea that grace has a saving effect: the historical act, or appearing, of grace in the coming of Jesus has brought about salvation (cf. vs. 14).

This saving concept, or better, person, is probably what we most readily associate with grace; we are saved by grace (Eph. 2:8). It is the act of regeneration when the Holy Spirit opens our eyes to our need for God, we put our faith in him, and he saves us.

Are you controlled by grace, so that you regularly, humbly acknowledge God's grace in your salvation? Are you regularly astounded by God's grace in remembering that he loves you not because of what you have done? Does this experience of God's grace lead to a longing to spread this good news of Jesus to the neighbors and coworkers in your life?

Notice what this saving grace produces: God's grace educates; it disciplines; it tutors (παιδεύουσα ἡμᾶς). The participle that begins verse 12 qualifies Ἐπεφάνη γὰρ ἡ χάρις τοῦ θεοῦ. God's saving grace is our life-coach. (See Galatians 3:24 for the parallel function of the Torah.) We are not, after experiencing grace, left alone to grope in the darkness of sin. The ἵνα clause in verse 12 provides the content and goal of grace's instruction: grace enables us to turn from sin (v. 12a negatively) and turn to activities that please God (vv. 12b–13 positively). In this present age marked by tension, grace instructs us to live godly lives, characterized by the fruit of the Holy Spirit (Gal. 3:3; 5:22–25).

Disciples of Jesus are to be controlled by grace. When grace is our companion, we have the power to say no to sinful choices. When grace is our companion, we become zealous for good works (ζηλωτὴν καλῶν ἔργων) in Jesus' name, which bring glory to God. When grace is our companion, we have the strength together to wait until Jesus appears again.

Sandwiched between Jesus first appearing and his future appearing, we are saved by God's grace, and we are to continue living by God's grace. Is this grace what makes you tick?

Joel Willitts and Jameson Ross

Persuasive Puns

Παρακαλῶ σε περὶ τοῦ ἐμοῦ τέκνου, ὃν ἐγέννησα ἐν τοῖς δεσμοῖς, Ὀνήσιμον, τόν ποτέ σοι ἄχρηστον νυνὶ δὲ [καὶ] σοὶ καὶ ἐμοὶ εὔχρηστον.... ναί, ἀδελφέ, ἐγώ σου ὀναίμην ἐν κυρίῳ· ἀνάπαυσόν μου τὰ σπλάγχνα ἐν Χριστῷ.

Many gems from Scripture come from paying careful attention to Greek grammar. But sometimes the benefits of knowing Greek come from such things as puns, double meanings, and wordplays. Two such puns are found in Paul's little jewel, his letter to Philemon. But Paul wasn't punning in order to have fun; his goal was to persuade Philemon to act in a way that befitted his profession of faith in Christ.

Paul was seeking to mediate a delicate situation between an old Christian friend (Philemon) and a new friend and child in the faith (Onesimus). Apparently Onesimus — formerly Philemon's slave — had run away from his master, Philemon. Somehow Onesimus ended up in prison with Paul, who introduced the fugitive to Christ (v. 10). After Onesimus believed, he ministered to Paul in prison (v. 13; cf. 11, 16). But both Paul and Onesimus knew that integrity required they contact Philemon about what had transpired before Onesimus believed; so Onesimus traveled toward Colossae, while holding tightly the letter Paul wrote to Philemon. In this letter, a reader of Greek encounters two connected puns.

Pun #1: Onesimus's name means "useful" or "beneficial."

Knowing this meaning makes verse 11 comprehensible: "Formerly he was useless [ἄχρηστον] to you, but now he is useful [εὔχρηστον] both to you and to me." It also explains why Paul employed a verbal form of Onesimus's own name in verse 20, "Yes, brother, let me benefit [ὀναίμην] from you in the Lord." That such punning was intended here is supported by Ignatius of Antioch's use of the same verb (ὀναίμην) fifty years later in a letter to the leader of the church in Ephesus who had the same name — Onesimus (possibly, though probably not the same Onesimus). By this pun Paul likely intended to build bridges with Philemon and empathetically introduce (vv. 10–11) and conclude (v. 20) the persuasive part of the letter. But there's more.

Pun #2: In verse 11 Greek speakers could easily have heard something that is untranslatable. χρηστός, from which the words ἄχρηστος and εὔχρηστος are derived, sounds so much like Χριστός ("Christ") that one must wonder whether Philemon wouldn't have heard an echo in ἄχρηστος that sounded something like ἀ-Χριστός ("without Christ"). In other words, Paul hints that formerly Onesimus was "without Christ," but now he is εὐ-Χριστός (or so the pun suggests), which may not mean anything in particular (since it is a pun, it doesn't have to), but it sounds very good (so "εὐ") and very Christian ("Χριστός").

In a passage written by the Roman historian Seutonius (*Life of Claudius* 25.4, in Latin), many historians believe he mixes up *Chrestus* (a fairly common name) with *Christus*, thus suggesting that such similarly pronounced words might include more than meets the eye. Paul's second pun takes the apostle's plea beyond simply saying that he who was formerly "useless" is now "useful"; it subtly Christianizes the discussion and may have led Philemon to be more sympathetic to Paul's plea. This furthering, of course, is all invisible to English-only speakers and readers.

Indeed, sensitive situations require delicate and wise words to resolve them. An appropriate pun can be employed when it promises to help move toward a Christian resolution. We do not know how Philemon responded to Paul's entreaties; but Paul's puns doubtlessly helped to soften the tension, engender empathy, and assist Philemon in hearing and responding to Paul's appeal.

Kenneth Berding

Πολυμερῶς καὶ πολυτρόπως πάλαι ὁ θεὸς λαλήσας τοῖς πατράσιν ἐν τοῖς προφήταις ἐπ᾽ ἐσχάτου τῶν ἡμερῶν τούτων <u>ἐλάλησεν</u> ἡμῖν ἐν υἱῷ.

I first saw my wife when I was substitute teaching a beginning Greek class in seminary. She was sitting on the front row. Over the next week I tried in vain to talk to her, but she kept leaving the class before I could initiate a conversation! Then, as I walked home from the library one day, I saw her working as a part of the grounds crew, and — miracle of miracles — she spoke to me. This encounter began a series of conversations that would change my life and lay the foundation for the big moment, five months later, when I asked Pat to marry me.

In Hebrews 1:1–2a the author starts with the miraculous news that God has initiated a conversation with us as human beings. (The passage can be diagrammed as follows with the main clause in bold typeface.) Notice the alliteration formed by words beginning with "π" and the parallelism built around the two uses of λαλέω (underlined):

> Πολυμερῶς καὶ πολυτρόπως
> πάλαι
> **ὁ θεός ...**
> <u>λαλήσας</u>

τοῖς πατράσιν
ἐν τοῖς προφήταις
ἐπ ἐσχάτου τῶν ἡμερῶν τούτων
ἐλάλησεν
ἡμῖν
ἐν υἱῷ

The first occurrence of God's "speaking" is an adverbial participle, λαλήσας; the second is the main verb, ἐλάλησεν. What is the relationship between these two words? How should we translate the text to show this relationship best, and what theological difference does the translation make?

Despite the fact that, in Greek, all of Hebrews 1:1–4 is one long sentence (a convention called "periodic" style), most English versions translate 1:1–2a as two sentences or as a compound sentence (with two coordinate independent clauses). For example:

HCSB: Long ago God spoke to the fathers by the prophets at different times and in different ways. In these last days, He has spoken to us by His Son.

ESV: Long ago, at many times and in many ways, God spoke to our fathers by the prophets, but in these last days he has spoken to us by his Son.

NLT: Long ago God spoke many times and in many ways to our ancestors through the prophets. But now in these final days, he has spoken to us through his Son.

Notice how these translations present the relationship between the participle and the main verb as either sequential (HCSB) or contrastive (ESV, NLT). What they do not do is reflect the participle's *dependence* on the verb, nor do they show the nature of that dependence.

One could argue that the adverbial participle should be understood as temporal ("after speaking ... God spoke" [e.g., NET, NASB]). But it is better to see it more generally as communicating the circumstances surrounding God's speaking to us through the Son: "having spoken ... God spoke ..."). This interpretation presents God's revelation during the Old Testament era as both the *foundation* of and the *preparation* for God's ultimate revelation through his Son, Jesus. While, to be sure, the two eras are different, the verbal ideas here emphasize the unity of God's revelation in both the Old and New Testaments as one single revelation from God.

This understanding provides one reason why it is so important for us to know the Old Testament and embrace it fully as Christian Scripture. God the Father used what we call the Old Testament to prepare for the moment when God the Son would step on earth, walk its roads, die, and be resurrected. In other words, in the Old Testament God started a conversation with us—one that would culminate in the great news that he would rather die than live without us.

George Guthrie

Consider Whom?

HEBREWS 10:24–25

Καὶ κατανοῶμεν ἀλλήλους εἰς παροξυσμὸν ἀγάπης καὶ καλῶν ἔργων, μὴ ἐγκαταλείποντες τὴν ἐπισυναγωγὴν ἑαυτῶν, καθὼς ἔθος τισίν, ἀλλὰ παρακαλοῦντες, καὶ τοσούτῳ μᾶλλον ὅσῳ βλέπετε ἐγγίζουσαν τὴν ἡμέραν.

One might assume from many English translations that the primary verb in Hebrews 10:24–25 is "to stimulate." However, the word rendered "stimulate" (παροξυσμός) is actually a noun. The main verb is "consider" (κατανοέω, cf. 3:1). Yet the injunction is not: "Consider how to love each other and do good deeds." That rendering would be biblical and right. But here the wording is different. Hebrews 10:24 says, "And let us consider *one another* to [εἰς followed by an accusative here connoting purpose] provoke love and good works" (cf. 6:10).

The direct object of the verb "consider" is the reciprocal pronoun, "one another." It is God's call for believers to consider one another — that is, to look at one another, think about one another, focus on one another, study one another, let minds be occupied with one another (see BDAG s.v. κατανοέω 2: "to think about carefully, envisage, think about, notice"). Thoughtful scrutiny is required. We are not to reach conclusions about each other quickly or casually. Rather, we must take time to understand each other and to figure out how best to approach each other's mutual needs for growth.

Because the noun παροξυσμός is such a potent word, English translators have felt justifiably compelled to give it a verbal rendering: "stimulate" (NASB), "spur" (NIV, NET), "stir up" (NKJV, ESV), "provoke" (KJV, NRSV), "motivate" (NLT), or "promote" (HCSB). The only other use of this noun in the New Testament appears in Acts 15:39, where Luke refers to a "sharp disagreement" between Paul and Barnabas. It occurs twice in the Septuagint, where in both instances it has negative connotations: "provocation" (Deut. 29:27 [Eng. 29:28]; Jer. 39:37 [Eng. 32:37]). By contrast, παροξυσμός bears a favorable connotation in Hebrews 10:24. The author may be using this term in an ironic fashion. In other words, rather than provoking one another to anger, think about *how* to provoke one another to love and good deeds.

The above statements find grammatical support in 10:25, which expands on 10:24. The two participial clauses in the present tense — μὴ ἐγκαταλείποντες τὴν ἐπισυναγωγὴν ἑαυτῶν ("not forsaking our meeting together") and ἀλλὰ παρακαλοῦντες ("but rather encouraging [one another]") — are subordinate to κατανοέω ("let us consider"), the hortatory subjunctive main verb (10:24). Hence, the author gives us two vitally important ways to "consider" the spiritual well-being of other believers: (1) by not shirking our God-given responsibility to gather together and (2) by encouraging one another in the Lord.

A parallel idea occurs in 3:13 (ἀλλὰ παρακαλεῖτε ἑαυτοὺς καθ᾽ ἑκάστην ἡμέραν, "but encourage one another every day"). It presupposes the gathering together of believers for ongoing mutual encouragement. In both 3:13 and 10:24, the verb παρακαλέω includes notions of warning and reproof as well as encouragement. Both nuances of this verb were necessary because these believers appear to have been discouraged, for various reasons, from gathering as Christian — reasons such as the threat of persecution (10:32–34).

Although many of us (in the Western world) may not be confronting the severe trials faced by the believers addressed in Hebrews, contemporary believers can become discouraged because of other struggles. Some face marital conflicts, others have heartaches over rebellious or spiritually indifferent children. Some face demotion, loss of a job, or various health problems. Many may wonder whether God truly cares for them. So the church needs believers who will consider one another and provoke one another to love, good works, regular fellowship, and mutual encouragement.

Keith Krell

How to Ask for Wisdom

JAMES 1:5–8

Εἰ δέ τις ὑμῶν λείπεται σοφίας, αἰτείτω παρὰ τοῦ διδόντος θεοῦ πᾶσιν ἀπλῶς καὶ μὴ ὀνειδίζοντος, καὶ δοθήσεται αὐτῷ. αἰτείτω δὲ ἐν πίστει, μηδὲν διακρινόμενος, ὁ γὰρ διακρινόμενος ἔοικεν κλύδωνι θαλάσσης ἀνεμιζομένῳ καὶ ῥιπιζομένῳ μὴ γὰρ οἰέσθω ὁ ἄνθρωπος ἐκεῖνος ὅτι λήμψεταί τι παρὰ τοῦ κυρίου, ἀνὴρ δίψυχος, ἀκατάστατος ἐν πάσαις ταῖς ὁδοῖς αὐτοῦ.

Wisdom is essential for leading a mature Christian life. Throughout Scripture, the wisdom that comes from God certainly includes knowledge and insight, but more importantly it relates to the practical outworking of one's faith in every sphere of life. A lack of godly wisdom has catastrophic effects for one's life—effects evidenced by damaged relationships, deteriorated integrity, undisciplined behavior, and the inability to endure well through trials and troubles. A life without wisdom is characterized by internal division and instability.

James intertwines the theme of wisdom with spiritual maturity, both of which are by-products of patient endurance resulting from a tested faith (1:2–4). A spiritually mature person is complete and does not lack any essential virtues. If you lack wisdom, however, you must ask God, who gives wisdom generously. Moreover, to receive wisdom from God, you must ask in faith without "doubting" (διακρινόμενος). The doubter is pictured like wind-driven ocean waves because such a person is "double-minded" (δίψυχος). In this message is an interesting play on words (*paronomasia*) that helps us better define how we are to ask for wisdom.

The words διακρινόμενος (1:6) and δίψυχος (1:8) each begin with the similar δι- sound, and both pertain to having *divided thoughts*. Διακρινόμενος, translated here as "doubting," may convey several senses based on contextual usage. Possible meanings include: "to make a distinction," "to differentiate," "to decide between options," and "to be at odds with oneself." The meaning becomes clearer when paired with δίψυχος, "double-minded"— a word James may have coined, since it does not occur in any earlier Greek writings and is only found in later Christian writings. When we take these two words together, the doubter is one torn between two options, unable to make a decision between trusting in God and trusting in something else. Furthermore, James illustrates the doubter (διακρινόμενος) as tossed about on the undulating waves of the sea (1:6) and concludes that the one with a divided heart and mind (δίψυχος) is unstable in all his or her ways (1:8). The emphasis is on the synonymous nature of words used to characterize the petitioner who doubts.

In this passage we can detect another wordplay, but this one contrasts the double-minded petitioner, in need of wisdom, with the single-minded God, who gives wisdom. James 1:5 characterizes the way that God gives wisdom as ἁπλῶς ("generously, single-mindedly") καὶ μὴ ὀνειδίζοντος ("not reproaching, not reprimanding"). The word ἁπλῶς occurs only here in the New Testament, but based on cognate terms it has been translated in the majority of English versions as "generously" or "liberally." Douglas Moo, however, argues that the cognate terms elsewhere are translated as "simple," "single," "sincere," and "integrity." Likewise, Peter Davids points out that the participle μὴ ὀνειδίζοντος used with ἁπλῶς conveys the meaning that God gives wisdom single-mindedly, "with no mental reservations"; therefore, James uses ἁπλῶς as the antithesis of δίψυχος—singleness of mind and intention versus double-minded uncertainty.

In other words, James instructs us to ask God for wisdom with a faith that does not waver, and God will answer with unwavering faithfulness. Let us ask God for wisdom with undivided confidence that he will lavish his wisdom on us graciously, with no reservations!

Alan S. Bandy

The Testing of Faith

Ἵνα τὸ δοκίμιον ὑμῶν τῆς πίστεως πολυτιμότερον χρυσίου τοῦ ἀπολλυμένου διὰ πυρὸς δὲ δοκιμαζομένου, εὑρεθῇ εἰς ἔπαινον καὶ δόξαν καὶ τιμὴν ἐν ἀποκαλύψει Ἰησοῦ Χριστοῦ.

Peter's readers rejoice greatly in their salvation—a salvation ready to be revealed in the last time (1:5–6). At the present time, he encourages them that rejoicing in the face of various trials (1:6) proves the genuineness of their faith, which results in praise, glory, and honor at the revelation of Christ (1:7).

Their faith is more valuable than gold—the most precious metal of the day. And part of the reason for this greater value is that even gold will perish, since it is part of a perishing world. In contrast to perishable riches, our inheritance is imperishable, uncorrupted, and unfading (1:4). This contrast between faith and gold is obvious in the context. Less obvious is what genuine faith and gold have in common.

Peter employs a wordplay in 1:7 that is generally obscured by English translations. The *genuineness* of faith is connected to the *refining* of fire by way of two Greek cognates: ὁ δοκίμιον and δοκιμαζομένου. The first word (τὸ δοκίμιον) is normally translated "genuineness" or "proved genuine," which refers to a positive outcome in the face of testing; it can also refer to the *process* of testing (BDAG). The second word (δοκιμαζομένου) refers to putting something to the test in order to determine its genuineness or to draw a conclusion on the basis of testing.

In other words, faith is shown to be genuine by enduring through various trials. Gold is tested "by fire" — the common practice of burning off impurities, resulting in pure gold. The parallel between faith and gold should now be clear: faith is proved genuine through various trials, just as gold is proved genuine through fire.

There is, however, a further implication. We know that gold is proved genuine through the burning off of impurities, as elements that do not belong are stripped away. The parallel between faith and gold in 1:7 suggests that the way in which faith is proved genuine is similar: impurities are stripped away. In this sense, suffering various trials is analogous to fire: while such suffering may be fierce and threatening, it has the power to purify. Just as gold is left standing while impure elements are burned away, so faith is left standing while impure elements are lost in the "fire" of suffering. Through suffering we discover the core, genuine substance of our faith.

Thus, in 1 Peter 1:7 we witness a Greek wordplay that draws both a contrast and a parallel between faith and gold. Genuine faith is more valuable than gold, but like gold, faith is made pure by passing through fire.

Constantine R. Campbell

Καὶ αὐτὸ τοῦτο δὲ σπουδὴν πᾶσαν παρεισενέγκαντες ἐπιχορηγήσατε ἐν τῇ πίστει ὑμῶν τὴν ἀρετήν, ἐν δὲ τῇ ἀρετῇ τὴν γνῶσιν, ἐν δὲ τῇ γνώσει τὴν ἐγκράτειαν, ἐν δὲ τῇ ἐγκρατείᾳ τὴν ὑπομονήν, ἐν δὲ τῇ ὑπομονῇ τὴν εὐσέβειαν, ἐν δὲ τῇ εὐσεβείᾳ τὴν φιλαδελφίαν, ἐν δὲ τῇ φιλαδελφίᾳ τὴν ἀγάπην. ταῦτα γὰρ ὑμῖν ὑπάρχοντα καὶ πλεονάζοντα οὐκ ἀργοὺς οὐδὲ ἀκάρπους καθίστησιν εἰς τὴν τοῦ κυρίου ἡμῶν Ἰησοῦ Χριστοῦ ἐπίγνωσιν.

The entire Christian life is characterized by reception. God gives, and we receive (cf. 1 Cor. 4:7). Everything we have is a gift received from God's hand.

Peter assumes this foundational characteristic in his second letter. He begins by highlighting our great, giving God and, by implication, our act of receiving. That God is the subject of the "bestowing" or "giving" in verses 3 and 4 is obvious. What is less obvious is the subject of the verb καθίστησιν in verse 8. What causes us to grow more intimate with Jesus? To answer this question we must look closely at both the context of the paragraph and its grammar.

First, the context. The flow of Peter's thinking is clear: God has given us everything we need to live for him (v. 3). He has called us to himself (v. 3) and has bestowed promises on us (v. 4) so that we will participate in his nature. This participation becomes the basis (γάρ) from which we make every effort to acquire the seven qualities listed in verses 5–7. In other words, God is the subject of everything we receive in Christ.

As to the grammar, the verb καθίστησιν is important because it is the only finite verb in verse 8 and only the second in this section. Almost all English translations of this verse suggest that "they," referring to the qualities of verses 5–8, is the subject of this verb, translated negatively as "to keep from" or positively as "cause to be." According to this rendering, the seven qualities listed are actors influencing a believer's relationship with Jesus.

But there is a better option. Qualities by themselves don't produce a state of effective knowing; God produces that state. When parsed, καθίστησιν is a present active indicative verb, third person singular. Most translations (NIV, NET, ESV, NASB) translate it the way they do because of the grammatical rule that neuter plurals take singular verbs. Thus, ταῦτα in verse 8 is taken as the subject of the verb. While grammatically possible, such a translation does not deal adequately with the context. It may be better to see as the subject a noun that is implied but not stated, namely, God.

Thus, an alternative translation reads: "When you are in the process of possessing and increasing these virtues, while not being useless and unproductive, *God* brings these things to pass in your pursuit of the knowledge of our Lord Jesus Christ." Reading the passage this way, we see that God is the Giver of everything we receive in Christ. God not only gives us everything we need; he also causes us to know Jesus by continual growth in the various qualities mentioned. We pursue all of them as God works them in us.

Peter begins his letter with a strong theological affirmation: God gives. We have received and continue to receive from him. The physical posture that should characterize believers is an open hand. Each day we have an opportunity to live our lives by making every effort to add to our faith the qualities of godliness, self-control, perseverance, and love. If we do, God will keep us growing in our relationship with Jesus.

Joel Willitts and Jameson Ross

Can a Christian Be Free from Sin?

1 JOHN 3:6, 9; 5:18

Πᾶς ὁ ἐν αὐτῷ μένων οὐχ ἁμαρτάνει· πᾶς ὁ ἁμαρτάνων
οὐχ ἑώρακεν αὐτὸν οὐδὲ ἔγνωκεν αὐτόν.... Πᾶς ὁ
γεγεννημένος ἐκ τοῦ θεοῦ ἁμαρτίαν οὐ ποιεῖ, ὅτι σπέρμα
αὐτοῦ ἐν αὐτῷ μένει καὶ οὐ δύναται ἁμαρτάνειν, ὅτι ἐκ
τοῦ θεοῦ γεγέννηται.... Οἴδαμεν ὅτι πᾶς ὁ γεγεννημένος
ἐκ τοῦ θεοῦ οὐχ ἁμαρτάνει, ἀλλ᾽ ὁ γεννηθεὶς ἐκ τοῦ θεοῦ
τηρεῖ αὐτόν, καὶ ὁ πονηρὸς οὐχ ἅπτεται αὐτοῦ.

One of the more nettlesome issues of Christian discipleship is the problem of ongoing sin. In some cases, Christians have been so confident in their sanctification that they've disregarded concerns about holiness. Others have given up altogether. Still others (early Gnostics) were not sure that deeds conducted in the flesh really mattered.

This subject is of keen interest to John. He writes clearly that Jesus came to destroy all sin (1 John 3:5b, 8b). Its destruction means initially that Jesus' substitutionary sacrifice "carried away" our sins (cf. John 1:29) and its punishment. But John has more in mind. Jesus himself is pure — there is no sin in him; since that is the case, his work also includes opposition to all sinfulness.

To make the point unmistakable, John says that whoever is truly in an intimate relationship with Christ "never sins" (1 John 3:6; see also 3:9 – 10; 5:18). Those born of God — those who have received the "seed" of God, who are children of God—should not sin. In fact, 3:9 makes the statement bold: such people *are not able to sin* because they have been born of God.

These bold statements have caused many Christians to struggle. *Does John's statement mean that perfect holiness is God's expectation for me?* We can initially dismiss the notion that John believes Christians can be sinless. In 1:8–2:1 (see also 5:16–17) he says just the opposite, and we must allow that he is not contradicting himself in chapter 3. Some have suggested that John is addressing different issues in 2:1 and 3:6–10. In the earlier section he is rejecting early Gnostics, who discounted ethics in their embrace of a "higher spirituality." In the present verses, however, he is presenting an ideal, a vision of Christian character that is godly and above reproach.

A helpful solution concentrates on the tenses of the verbs. In Greek a present tense (in certain forms) indicates continuous, repeated activity. Four key texts are important. (1) In 3:6a and 5:18 John says that Christians "do not sin." The verb ἁμαρτάνω appears in the present indicative, and the sense is that we should not have the ongoing, self-endorsing habit of sin. (2) In 3:6b John uses a present participle ("those who continue to sin") to express the same notion. Once again, such a participle implies ongoing activity. (3) In 3:9a a different verb is used ("*to do* sin"), and sin appears as a noun. Again, the verb is a present tense. (4) Finally, in 3:9b John describes Christians as not "able to sin." Both δύναται ("to be able") and the infinitive ἁμαρτάνειν ("to sin") are present tense. Consequently, John may well be saying that ongoing, habitual sin should find no place in the believer's life.

John seems to be confronting people who say that Christians are *free to sin* (since they claim ethics are irrelevant). In John's warning in 3:7, the real subject is the *permissibility* of sin or a sort of metaphysical perfectionism that dismisses morality.

John emphasizes that what we do in this life matters. What

we do with our bodies matters since "matter matters" to God. So holiness counts, and those who separate their spiritual life from their creaturely life (claiming righteousness for one and disregarding the other) cannot fully understand what it means to love God.

Gary M. Burge

Fight for the Faith

JUDE 3

Ἀγαπητοί, πᾶσαν σπουδὴν ποιούμενος γράφειν ὑμῖν περὶ τῆς κοινῆς ἡμῶν σωτηρίας ἀνάγκην ἔσχον γράψαι ὑμῖν παρακαλῶν ἐπαγωνίζεσθαι τῇ ἅπαξ παραδοθείσῃ τοῖς ἁγίοις πίστει.

The letter Jude writes here is not the letter he originally intended. He had wanted to encourage his audience of believers to live Christian lives. But unfortunately, he discovered that evil people had crept into the church, so Jude emphasizes instead that God's people are to "fight hard for the faith once for all delivered to the saints."

Jude's description of these people is scathing. They were "shepherds feeding themselves" (v. 12) instead of the flock—a clear indication that these imposters were in leadership positions. Specifically, they were teaching that sanctification didn't matter, thus perverting "the grace of our God into sensuality"; they were also deficient in their Christology, as evidence by their denial of "our only Master and Lord, Jesus Christ" (v. 4).

It is sad when a church experiences the truth of Paul's prophecy that "fierce wolves will come in among you, not sparing the flock" (Acts 20:29). I find myself welcoming opposition from outside the church, because the church can bind together against a common enemy. The spiritual warfare that exists inside a church, however, is much more insidious and more difficult to fight.

So what does Jude recommend? Part of his answer is found in the verb ἐπαγωνίζομαι in verse 3. The main portion of this verb is ἀγωνίζομαι, which can mean to take part in an athletic contest (1 Cor. 9:25) or, in a more general sense, to fight or struggle (either physically [e.g., John 18:23] or metaphorically [e.g., Col. 4:12; 2 Tim. 4:7]). Often the preposition ἐπί, when attached to a verb, intensifies the notion of struggle. Thus both Louw and Nida and BDAG offer the nuance "to exert intense effort on behalf of something."

So, those translations that merely use "contend" (e.g., ESV, NIV, NRSV) seem too weak. The NASB and NET are more on track with "contend earnestly" (cf. KJV). NJB has "fight hard," which is the best translation. Jude is telling the church that the time has come to take off the kid gloves and duke it out. This is not the time for caution and reserve. It is war. We must be ready to wage fierce battles within the body.

I can remember when, as fulltime pastor, I was informed about a questionable doctrine being taught by some of our youth teachers. These people were good, likeable people. But working through Jude, where I saw when and how we should deal with false teaching, convinced me that I could not ignore or even deal gently with this situation. So I preached a three-part series on Jude, established a biblical policy on dealing with false teaching, and gave these teachers a chance to talk with the council. When they did not change their minds, we released them from service.

Was taking this action going too far? Perhaps so in a society in which the prevailing attitude is, "You are entitled to your own opinion, and I am to mine." But not in the church! Biblical teachings about Christ and the effect they have on our lives are so central that to ignore them leaves us with a faith that does not agree with the faith once-for-all delivered to the saints. The process is not pleasant, but Jude says that we must at times "fight hard" for the faith — faith defined here as the core of the gospel of salvation, not varying interpretations of any unclear passages of the Bible.

William D. Mounce

The One Who Is, the One Who Was, and the One Who Is Coming

Ἰωάννης ταῖς ἑπτὰ ἐκκλησίαις ταῖς ἐν τῇ Ἀσίᾳ· χάρις ὑμῖν καὶ εἰρήνη ἀπὸ ὁ ὢν καὶ ὁ ἦν καὶ ὁ ἐρχόμενος, καὶ ἀπὸ τῶν ἑπτὰ πνευμάτων ἃ ἐνώπιον τοῦ θρόνου αὐτοῦ.

Sometimes the most significant feature of a passage in the Greek New Testament occurs when rules of grammar are broken. Rough-hewn phrases force the reader to pause and wonder why the writer has departed from the expected grammar. These improprieties are called solecisms. Revelation 1:4 represents the first of twenty-seven solecisms in Revelation. There are several oddities about the phrase ἀπὸ ὁ ὢν καὶ ὁ ἦν καὶ ὁ ἐρχόμενος, but the most striking incongruity is a nominative participle (ὁ ὢν) following the preposition ἀπό. Normally, of course, ἀπό takes its object in the genitive. The effect of this reading would be jarring because of the unexpected shift in case. This grammatical dissonance would be as if someone said, "Where was you at?" You know what the person is saying, but you cringe at their poor grammar. What could be the purpose for John's poor grammar?

Two possible options may explain the reason for John's solecisms. He may be *unintentionally* making grammatical mistakes because his native language is Aramaic and he does not know Greek grammar well enough. This view, however, ignores the fact that, overall, Revelation is written in fairly good Greek. In all other occurrences in Revelation John correctly uses the genitive case after ἀπό. In other words, John did indeed know Greek well enough to avoid this mistake.

The second option, then, is that John *intentionally* diverged from correct grammar for a reason. Greg Beale, in his magisterial commentary on Revelation, observes that all twenty-seven solecisms introduce allusions to Old Testament texts. Revelation 1:4 alludes to the Greek version of Exodus 3:14, where God reveals his personal name to Moses: ἐγώ εἰμι ὁ ὤν ("I am the one who is"). John breaks the rules of Greek grammar because he wants to preserve the name of God when indicating that the source of his vision is ἀπὸ ὁ ὤν ("from the one who is"). Yet John not only preserves God's name; he also expands it to stress God's eternality by adding "the one who was, and the one who is coming." In other words, God is now, God was in the past, and God will be in the future—he is the eternal, ever-present God.

This awkward phrase emphasizes the name of God and his eternal transcendence over time. John uses this name for God again in 1:8, along with the titles "the Alpha and Omega" and "the Almighty." Not only is God the One who exists throughout time and eternity, but he is also the all-powerful sovereign Lord who controls the beginning and end of history. Revelation is a book for persecuted believers living in a hostile, pagan environment; it describes the victorious return of Christ and the consummation of his kingdom on earth. It is no accident, then, that John begins by presenting God as the Eternal One who is always present with his people, just as he was with them in the past and will be in the future.

You may find yourself facing challenging situations, such as unemployment, medical problems, ostracism, opposition to your faith, or some other trial. You will find strength to endure when you remember that the same God who was faithful to Abraham, Moses, and David is the same God who is with you, now and forever. The God who transcends time and controls history can most certainly see you through your struggles.

Alan S. Bandy

When Forgiveness Is a Sin

Ἀλλὰ ἔχω κατὰ σοῦ ὅτι ἀφεῖς τὴν γυναῖκα Ἰεζάβελ.

It is hard to think of a book that has captured the fascination and emotions of its readers as much as the Apocalypse of John. When the God of our universe ripped open the sky and the Lord Jesus Christ appeared at the height of his glory before John, the man on Patmos stood awestruck by the vision (Rev. 1:17). In chapters 2–3, this same glorious Jesus strips away all pretense when he exposes, one by one, the true spiritual condition of seven churches in Asia Minor. Among Christ's many exhortations, his address to the church at Thyatira is the most sobering (2:18–29).

Though the Thyatiran Christians are commended for their works of love, faith, ministry, and perseverance (v. 19), Jesus nevertheless faults them severely for their failure to confront the false prophetess Jezebel, who wrongly taught the permissibility of eating food sacrificed to idols. "But I have (this) against you," says the risen Lord, "that *you are forgiving* [ἀφεῖς] the woman Jezebel" (v. 20). Many Bible translations (e.g., NIV, TNIV, ESV, NRSV) render the Greek verb ἀφεῖς as "you tolerate." Yet if we consider the various definitions of ἀφίημι, "tolerate" is a weak choice. A quick look at any Greek lexicon, such as BDAG, gives several possible meanings for ἀφίημι, including: "1. send away; 2. forgive; 3. abandon; 4. leave lying around; or 5. allow, tolerate."

It is an exegetical mistake, of course, to assume that all these meanings are operational in this single occurrence of the verb. (Such an error is known as an "illegitimate totality transfer.") Neither should the translator randomly choose just any definition; rather, given the semantic range of ἀφίημι, the biblical interpreter needs to decide which meaning best fits the literary context. In 2:20–21, the context of Christ's address to Thyatira is clearly repentance. Christ claims that he gave Jezebel "time to repent" (χρόνον ἵνα μετανοήσῃ; v. 21a) but laments that "she is unwilling to repent" (οὐ θέλει μετανοῆσαι; v. 21b). He desperately warns of impending physical judgment unless she and her followers "repent from her works" (ἐὰν μὴ μετανοήσωσιν ἐκ τῶν ἔργων αὐτῆς; v. 22). Since μετανοέω is used three times in the span of just two verses, translating ἀφίημι as "forgive" becomes the obvious and preferred choice.

Thus Jesus warns the church: "You are forgiving [ἀφεῖς] the woman Jezebel," when she should *not* be forgiven. Since Jezebel "willfully refuses to repent" (a translation that brings out better the force of οὐ θέλει), the church has no business pardoning her—or anyone whom Christ has not pardoned. The warning is reminiscent of Jesus' commission in John 20:23: "If you forgive [ἀφῆτε] the sins of any, they are forgiven [ἀφέωνται]; if you hold sins against anyone, they are held (against him or her)." Christ calls every congregation to discern whether members have truly repented. It is the church's priestly duty to act as mediators, to speak for God, and *not* to forgive if persons like the Thyatiran Jezebel continue willfully and eagerly to sin (cf. Matt. 18:15–18).

Of course, such authority becomes hurtful if misused. The Christian community should not abuse its power. Instead, with maturity, wisdom, and courage, the followers of Jesus must venture to name sin when it is present, but also—with blood, sweat, tears, and prayer—help sinners experience the forgiveness of God. Grace demands that we never let sin go unchecked, or sin will ruin lives. Yet at the same time, grace demands that we make every call to repentance a genuine expression of love for the other.

Max J. Lee

Focusing Attention on Christ

Καὶ ἦλθεν καὶ εἴληφεν ἐκ τῆς δεξιᾶς τοῦ καθημένου ἐπὶ τοῦ θρόνου.

These words are part of a stirring scene near the beginning of Revelation where the Lamb appears in heaven to receive a scroll (probably containing God's plan to establish his kingdom). The most interesting grammatical feature in 5:7 is the use of the perfect-tense form εἴληφεν (from λαμβάνω) as Christ takes the scroll from God's right hand. This perfect tense comes in the middle of, and breaks the pattern of, a string of aorist tenses in verses 7–8 (ἦλθεν, ἔλαβεν, ἔπεσαν).

So why the perfect tense here? The usual understanding of the perfect in the New Testament is that it communicates "existing results" or a "state." But here many find it difficult to translate the perfect with its full force of "existing results" ("he came and now he has taken the scroll"). A common explanation for 5:7, therefore, appeals to a category found in most of our grammars called the "aoristic perfect" or "dramatic perfect." In this usage, often found in narration, the perfect tense can function like an aorist and merely denote past action: "he took."

But does this translation do justice to the perfect εἴληφεν in Revelation 5:7? First, notice that the next verb after εἴληφεν is ἔλαβεν in verse 8 — the aorist of the same verb, λαμβάνω! In fact, λαμβάνω occurs twice more as an *aorist* infinitive (λαβεῖν, vv. 9, 12). If εἴληφεν is truly an aoristic perfect, why did John change to the aorist of the same verb in the next verse? John's choice of the perfect in 5:7 seems deliberate and should retain its force, even if we cannot easily capture it in English.

If we ask why John might have chosen the perfect εἴληφεν, it is helpful to recall that the Greek verbal tenses sometimes function to highlight or give prominence to certain actions in the discourse — that is, they can have a "discoursive" function. In narrative the aorist is the usual, background tense that carries the story along. The present tense (so-called "historical/narrative present") draws attention to certain actions against the backdrop of the aorist verbs. But when an author wants to focus even greater attention on selected actions or features of the story, they can use the weightier perfect tense.

- aorist: background
- present: highlighting
- perfect: special focus

In the light of these functions, the perfect tense in Revelation 5:7 is significant! John has chosen εἴληφεν to focus special attention on this particular act of the Lamb as he takes the scroll from the hand of God. This action is the climax of the whole vision and the ultimate answer to John's despair that no one was found worthy to open the scroll (5:3–4). Someone *was found worthy* to take the scroll! Consequently, the author wants us to sit up and take notice, so he marks this act with the perfect tense! The effect is like shining the spotlight on the main hero in the last scene of a play. Christ now takes center stage and performs what no one else can do. Here is the event we, the audience, have been waiting for.

In other words, John's use of the perfect tense helps us to focus attention on Christ as the center of God's plan for redemption and salvation. No one else can take the scroll and set its contents in motion! No wonder the creatures and elders (vv. 9–10), then throngs of angels (v. 12), and eventually the entire creation (v. 13) break out in worship of the Lamb! How can we remain unmoved and fail to do likewise?

David L. Mathewson

The Authors

Alan S. Bandy: Alan S. Bandy (PhD, Southeastern Baptist Theological Seminary) is Rowena R. Strickland Chair of Bible and Assistant Professor of New Testament and Greek at Oklahoma Baptist University in Shanwee, Oklahoma. He is coauthoring *The Theology of Revelation* with Andreas J. Köstenberger for the Zondervan Biblical Theology of the New Testament series.

Linda Belleville: Linda Belleville (PhD, St. Michael's College, University of Toronto) is Professor of New Testament at Bethel College and Graduate School in Mishawaka, Indiana. She is the author of *Women Leaders and the Church: 3 Crucial Questions* and *2 Corinthians* in the IVP New Testament commentary series.

Kenneth Berding: Kenneth Berding (PhD, Westminster Theological Seminary) is Professor of New Testament at Biola University, Talbot School of Theology, in La Mirada, California. He is the author of *Polycarp and Paul: An Analysis of their Literary and Theological Relationship in Light of Polycarp's Use of Biblical and Extra-Biblical Literature* and the audio CD, *Sing and Learn New Testament Greek.*

Craig L. Blomberg: Craig L. Blomberg (PhD, University of Aberdeen) is Distinguished Professor of New Testament at Denver Seminary. He is the author, coauthor, or coeditor of fifteen books and more than eighty articles in journals or multiauthor works.

Darrell L. Bock: Darrell L. Bock (PhD, University of Aberdeen) is Professor of New Testament studies at Dallas Theological Seminary. He is coeditor and a contributor to *Dispensationalism, Israel and the Church* and author of the NIV Application Commentary on *Luke.*

Gary M. Burge: Gary M. Burge (PhD, University of Aberdeen) is a professor in the Department of Bible, Theology, Archaeology, and World Religions at Wheaton College in Illinois. He is the author of *John* and *Letters of John* in the NIV Application Commentary series and is coauthor with Lynn Cohick and Gene Green of *The New Testament in Antiquity.*

Constantine R. Campbell: Constantine R. Campbell (PhD, Macquarie University) is a senior lecturer in Greek and New Testament at Moore Theological College in Sydney, Australia. He is the author of *Basics of Verbal Aspect in Biblical Greek* and *Paul and Union with Christ.*

Roy E. Ciampa: Roy E. Ciampa (PhD, University of Aberdeen) is Professor of New Testament at Gordon-Conwell Theological Seminary in South Hamilton, Massachusetts. He has published with Brian Rosner the commentary on *The First Letter to the Corinthians* in the Pillar commentary series.

Lynn H. Cohick: Lynn H. Cohick (PhD, University of Pennsylvania) is Associate Professor of New Testament in the Department of Biblical and Theological Studies at Wheaton College and Graduate School in Illinois. She has written on early Jewish/Christian relations in her book, *Melito of Sardis: Setting, Purpose, and Sources* (Brown Judaic Studies, 2000). She is a coauthor with Gary Burge and Gene Green of *The New Testament in Antiquity.*

Dean B. Deppe: Dean B. Deppe (PhD, Free University of Amsterdam) has been the Professor of New Testament Theology at Calvin Theological Seminary since 1998. His most recent book (2011) is entitled, *All Roads Lead to the Text: Eight Methods of Inquiry into the Bible.*

J. R. Dodson: J. R. Dodson (PhD, University of Aberdeen) is Assistant Professor of Biblical Studies at Ouachita Baptist University in Arkedelphia, Arkansas. He is the author of *The "Powers"* *of Personification: Rhetorical Purpose in the "Book of Wisdom" and the Letter to the Romans.*

J. Scott Duvall: J. Scott Duvall (PhD, Southwestern Baptist Theological Seminary) is Professor of New Testament at Ouachita Baptist University. He is coauthor with J. Daniel Hays of the hermeneutics textbook *Grasping God's Word: A Hands-on Approach to Reading, Interpreting, and Applying the Bible.*

George H. Guthrie: George H. Guthrie (PhD, Southwestern Baptist Theological Seminary) is Benjamin W. Perry Professor of Bible at Union University in Jackson, Tennessee. He is the author of *Hebrews* in the NIV Application Commentary series and coauthor, with J. Scott Duvall, of *Biblical Greek Exegesis.*

Paul Jackson: Paul Jackson (PhD, Southwestern Baptist Theological Seminary) is Professor of Biblical Studies at Union University in Jackson, Tennessee. He is the author of *An Investigation of Koimaomai in the New Testament: The Concept of Eschatological Sleep.*

Edward W. Klink III: Edward W. Klink III (PhD, University of St. Andrews) is Associate Professor of New Testament at Biola University, Talbot School of Theology, in La Mirada, California. He is the author of *The Sheep of the Fold: The Audience and Origin of the Gospel of John* and is currently writing a commentary on the gospel of *John* for the Zondervan Exegetical Commentary on the New Testament series.

Keith Krell: Keith Krell (PhD, University of Bristol) is Pastor of Emmanuel Bible Fellowship Church in Olympia, Washington and Adjunct Professor of Biblical Studies for Moody Bible Institute in Spokane, Washington. Keith's writings are available at timelessword.com.

Max J. Lee: Max J. Lee (PhD, Fuller Theological Seminary) is Associate Professor of New Testament at North Park Theological

Seminary. He is currently working on the monograph *Moral Transformation in Greco-Roman Philosophy of Mind* for Mohr-Siebeck's WUNT series. He is an ordained Baptist minister.

Michelle Lee-Barnewall: Michelle Lee-Barnewall (PhD, University of Notre Dame) is Associate Professor of Biblical and Theological Studies at Talbot School of Theology of Biola University. She is the author of *Paul, the Stoics, and the Body of Christ* (Cambridge, 2006).

Gary Manning Jr.: Gary Manning Jr. (PhD, Fuller Theological Seminary) is Associate Professor of New Testament at Biola University, Talbot School of Theology, in La Mirada, California. He is the author of *Echoes of a Prophet: The Use of Ezekiel in the Gospel of John and in Literature of the Second Temple Period.*

David L. Mathewson: David L. Mathewson (PhD, University of Aberdeen) is Associate Professor of New Testament at Denver Seminary. He has written *Verbal Aspect in the Book of Revelation,* and *A New Heaven and a New Earth: The Meaning and Function of the Old Testament in Revelation 21:1–22:5.*

Scot McKnight: Scot McKnight (PhD, Nottingham University) is Karl A. Olsson Professor of Religious Studies at North Park University, in Chicago. He is the author of several books, including *Galatians* and *1 Peter* in the NIV Application Commentary series, and the award-winning *The Jesus Creed.*

William D. Mounce: William D Mounce (PhD, University of Aberdeen) lives as a writer in Washougal, Washington. He is President of BiblicalTraining.org, a nonprofit organization offering world-class educational resources for discipleship in the local church. He is the author of the bestselling Greek textbook, *Basics of Biblical Greek*, and many other resources.

C. Marvin Pate: C. Marvin Pate (PhD, Marquette University) chairs the Department of Christian Theology and is Professor of

Theology at Ouachita Baptist University in Arkedelphia, Arkansas. He has authored, coauthored, or edited twenty books.

Mark Strauss: Mark Strauss (PhD, University of Aberdeen) is Professor of New Testament at Bethel Seminary in San Diego. He is the author of *Four Portraits, One Jesus* and the coauthor of *The Challenge of Bible Translation* and *Gender Accuracy*. He is currently writing a commentary on the gospel of Mark for the Zondervan Exegetical Commentary on the New Testament Series.

Verlyn D. Verbrugge: Verlyn D. Verbrugge (PhD, University of Notre Dame) is Senior Editor-at-Large for Biblical and Theological Resources at Zondervan. He abridged the *New International Dictionary of New Testament Theology* and is the author of *A Not-So-Silent Night: The Unheard Story of Christmas and Why It Matters*.

David Wallace: David Wallace (PhD, Southwestern Baptist Theological Seminary) teaches Greek and New Testament courses as an adjunct instructor at Southwestern Baptist Theological Seminary and is Pastor of Dean Baptist Church in Tyler, Texas. He is the author of the *Gospel of God: Romans as Paul's Aeneid*.

Matt Williams: Matt Williams (PhD, Trinity International University) is Professor of Biblical and Theological Studies at Biola University, Talbot School of Theology, in La Mirada, California. He served six years as a missionary professor to the Spanish Bible Institute and Seminary in Barcelona, Spain. He is an editor and contributor for the Deeper Connections series: *The Parables of Jesus, The Miracles of Jesus*, and *The Prayers of Jesus*.

Joel L. Willitts: Joel L. Willitts (PhD, Cambridge University) is Associate Professor in Biblical and Theological Studies at North Park University in Chicago. He is the author of *Matthew's Messianic Shepherd-King: In Search of "The Lost Sheep of the House* *of Israel,"* and *The Kregel Pictorial Guide to the Dead Sea Scrolls: How They Were Discovered and What They Mean.* Jameson Ross is a pastor along with Joel at Christ Community Church and is an MA student in the Exegesis program at Wheaton Graduate School.

Mark W. Wilson: Mark W. Wilson (DLitt et Phil., University of South Africa), a former adjunct professor of New Testament at Regent University in Virginia Beach, Virginia, is currently serving at the Asia Minor Research Center in Antalya, Turkey. He wrote the commentary on *Revelation* in the Zondervan Illustrated Bible Backgrounds Commentary series.

Ben Witherington III: Ben Witherington III (PhD, University of Durham) is professor of New Testament at Asbury Theological Seminary. Considered one of the leading evangelical scholars in the world, he has authored or coauthored over forty books, including *The Brother of Jesus, The Jesus Quest,* and *The Paul Quest.*

A Reader's Greek New Testament

2nd Edition

*Richard J. Goodrich and
Albert L. Lukaszewski*

Ideal for Greek students and
pastors, *A Reader's Greek New
Testament* saves time and effort in
studying the Greek New Testament. By eliminating the need
to look up definitions, the footnotes allow the user to read the
Greek text more quickly, focusing on parsing and grammatical
issues. This revised edition offers the following features:

- New Greek font—easier to read
- Footnoted definitions of all Greek words occurring 30
  times or less
- Mini-lexicon of all words occurring more than 30 times
- Greek text underlying Today's New International
  Version
- Footnotes offering comparisons with UBS4
- 4 pages of full-color maps

Featuring a handsome Italian Duo-Tone™ binding, *A
Reader's Greek New Testament*, 2nd Edition is a practical, attractive, and surprisingly affordable resource.

Available in stores and online!

ZONDERVAN®
.com

Keep Your Greek

Strategies for Busy People

Constantine R. Campbell

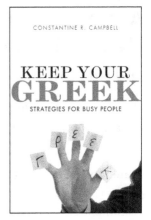

Seminarians spend countless hours mastering biblical languages and learning how the knowledge of them illuminates the reading, understanding, and application of Scripture. But while excellent language acquisition resources abound, few really teach students how to maintain their use of Greek for the long term. Consequently, as pastors and other former Greek students find that under the pressures of work, ministry, preaching, and life, their hard-earned Greek skills begin to disappear.

Con Campbell has been counseling one-time Greek students for years, teaching them how to keep their language facility for the benefit of those to whom they minister and teach. He shows how following the right principles makes it possible for many to retain—and in some cases regain—their Greek language skills.

Pastors will find *Keep Your Greek* an encouraging and practical guide to strengthening their Greek abilities so that they can make linguistic insights a regular part of their study and teaching. Current students will learn how to build skills that will serve them well once they complete their formal language instruction.

Available in stores and online!

Biblical Greek: A Compact Guide

William D. Mounce

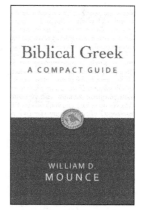

Biblical Greek: A Compact Guide offers Greek students a one-stop guide for the grammar, morphology, and vocabulary of biblical Greek in a handy size. This resource follows the organization and format familiar to the hundreds of thousands of students who have used *Basics of Biblical Greek Grammar* in their first-year Greek courses, but it is also usable by students who learned with a different grammar. By limiting its discussion to the "nuts and bolts," Greek language students working on translation and exegesis will more quickly and easily find the relevant grammatical refreshers.

Students can, for example, check on the range of meaning for a particular word or make sure they remember how aorist participles function in a sentence. The paradigms, word lists, and basic discussions in *Biblical Greek: A Compact Guide* point students in the right direction and allow them to focus on more advanced Greek study.

Biblical Greek: A Compact Guide will become a valuable addition to the reference library of seminary students and pastors.

Available in stores and online!

Greek Grammar Beyond the Basics

An Exegetical Syntax of the New Testament

Daniel B. Wallace

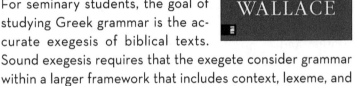

For seminary students, the goal of studying Greek grammar is the accurate exegesis of biblical texts. Sound exegesis requires that the exegete consider grammar within a larger framework that includes context, lexeme, and other linguistic features.

While the trend of some grammarians has been to take a purely grammatical approach to the language, *Greek Grammar Beyond the Basics* integrates the technical requirements for proper Greek interpretation with the actual interests and needs of Bible students. It is the first textbook to systematically link syntax and exegesis of the New Testament for second-year Greek students. It explores numerous syntactical categories, some of which have not previously been dealt with in print.

Greek Grammar Beyond the Basics is the most up-to-date Greek grammar available. It equips intermediate Greek students with the skills they need to do exegesis of biblical texts in a way that is faithful to their intended meaning. The expanded edition contains a subject index, a Greek word index, and page numbers in the Syntax Summary section.

Available in stores and online!

NIV Greek and English New Testament

John R. Kohlenberger III, General Editor

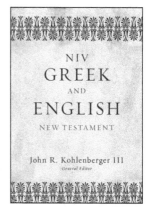

The *NIV Greek and English New Testament* is a parallel Bible, with the Greek New Testament on the left-hand page (using the text that underlies the NIV 2011) and the NIV 2011 on the right-hand page. The Greek text includes footnotes that relate to other Greek New Testaments, and the NIV has the footnotes readers have come to expect and rely on. Section headings are identical in both editions for easy reference.

Additional features of the *NIV Greek and English New Testament* include:

- Side-by-side format (Greek text on one page with NIV on the facing page)
- Greek text formatted to match the NIV text
- Single column format
- Words of Christ in black
- Presentation page
- Ribbon marker (leather edition only)
- Maps

Available in stores and online!

ZONDERVAN®
.com

Printed in the USA
CPSIA information can be obtained
at www.ICGtesting.com
JSHW011705130124
55277JS00014B/156